HOW TO CATCH
A MOLE

Marc Hamer

HOW TO
CATCH
A MOLE

And Find Yourself in Nature

Harvill *Secker*
LONDON

1 3 5 7 9 10 8 6 4 2

Harvill Secker, an imprint of Vintage,
20 Vauxhall Bridge Road,
London SW1V 2SA

Harvill Secker is part of the Penguin Random House group of companies
whose addresses can be found at global.penguinrandomhouse.com

'4 a.m.' and an early version of 'Driving narrow lanes by curly bracken
banks' first published in The Lonely Crowd, issue 8. 2018

Illustrations by Joe McLaren

First published by Harvill Secker in 2019

A CIP catalogue record for this book is available from the British Library

penguin.co.uk/vintage

ISBN 9781787301245

Typeset in 13/18 pt Adobe Jenson Pro
by Integra Software Services Pvt. Ltd, Pondicherry

Printed and bound in Great Britain by Clays Ltd, Elcograf S.p.A.

Penguin Random House is committed to a sustainable future for
our business, our readers and our planet. This book is made
from Forest Stewardship Council® certified paper.

For Kate
(Peggy)
To whom I owe everything

There is a man who haunts the forest,
that hangs odes upon hawthorns and elegies on
    brambles.

As You Like It, Act III, Scene 2

I love my Peggy's angel air
Her face so truly, heavenly fair
Her native grace so void of art
But I adore my Peggy's heart.

Robbie Burns

Sunday I'll go molecatching
hang their smooth soft bodies
from the thorns
where farmers can see my work
and shiny crows can gorge.

Contents

Prologue

I am a gardener. I have been catching moles in gardens and farms for years, and I have decided that I am not going to do it any more. Molecatching is a traditional skill that has given me a good life, but I am old now and tired of hunting, trapping and killing, and it has taught me what I needed to learn.

To protect their livelihood, molecatchers have always kept their knowledge hidden. I don't want to let that tradition disappear, so in this book I am going tell you about the behaviour of moles and how to catch them, should you want to do so, and a little about what you can do instead. Wrapped around this tradition is the story of the mole itself, and also of my life as a molecatcher: what that life was like, the long route to getting there, how it affected me, and why eventually I decided to stop.

I feel some conflict about stopping. To the core of my being I love the life that I have been given. A life that encourages a passion for nature, for its functional beauty and its violent brutal energy – even for its decay. It has been a reflective life that has affected my view of the wider world and how to live in it. It changed my relationship with myself, with my personal history and with my family. So here there are fragments of my life, too, and some of the things that led me to becoming a molecatcher.

Each telling of any story seems different, and this is true of my own life. When I was sixteen I left home and started walking. I walked for about eighteen months, and lived wild with the animals and birds, sleeping under hedges, in woodlands and on riverbanks. I will try to be as truthful as possible about this too, but not all the facts are clear. There is much that I can't remember. Sometimes the two stories of mole and me seem to be inextricably intertwined. There are echoes and reflections. But the dance between these two vague tales has become a way of living that I find simple and beautiful and has given me everything that I could ever want.

I wonder about truth and what it is as I chase it around and play with it. Recollections rarely come in chronological order. Memory wanders in the darkness, and the harder I try to remember, the more it seems to dissolve in front of me and take a different direction. As soon as I start to examine a story with anything more intense than a sidelong glance, it shifts in reaction to the scrutiny, reconstructs itself and then changes again, like looking into a kaleidoscope: the colours are identical, their patterns slightly different every time, their detail constantly changes yet the picture remains true to itself.

All the facts that I recall easily are just high points and low ones, bits remembered only because they have some emotional impact or connection to something seen or remembered. They are like a string of pearls: tarnished pearls that have been shut in a drawer and rarely taken out. As I pull them out and look at them some of them are missing, and life seems like mostly string without a pearl in sight – and then a cluster of them appear, tangled and out of sequence.

There is no certainty there, and yet, I will try to unravel the strands.

Often I do not disturb myself with language and I just look and enjoy. At other times words come silently creeping in on insect legs. Some start to build a nest, develop a theme – a twig here, a bud there – so I let them. I like to write bits, tiny bits of stuff that fly by like leaves, insubstantial, scattering, and could be gone if I didn't grab them out of the air. Bits of ordinary stuff that I see and that I can hold in my head in their entirety. Like individual memories or the fragments of pottery that I find in the molehills. Here – alongside and flowing sometimes in and around the simple yet often bizarre facts about how to catch a mole – are these fragments, sometimes sharp, sometimes smooth, written for the most part while wandering across a field with a bag of traps.

Telling the whole story of the life of a mole is equally impossible. Hidden in the darkness, his story is created from myths and a handful of observations passed on from person to person, each with their own point of view. The moles, like us, are deeply mysterious creatures, and we will only ever catch a glimpse of their truth.

What things seem to be matters far more to me than what things actually are. What they actually are is unknowable. I don't like that prison of hard and cold facts. Facts do not set you free, they trap you into a constructed view of reality that is final. The only truth is here, and here, and here in the three seconds before it becomes a reconstruction. Really I want to forget. Forgetting is freedom and forgiveness but more than anything it is a process of immersing myself in what is happening now.

I could tell this story with myself as the villain or the hero, innocent bystander or agent provocateur, and each time I'd be telling a form of the 'truth'. What is the value of a truth that has an infinite number of forms? There is a difference between truth and honesty, so I am going to tell you one of the millions of honest stories that I could tell you that might be good enough to call 'true'. One of the stories that led me to the point of kneeling in a muddy field in

December with a dead mole in my hand and deciding it was time to stop killing.

How to catch a mole, life as a molecatcher. Written in the season of catching moles, instead of catching moles. I think the only certainty I can give you about this book is that by the end you will know a lot more about moles.

Daybreak

As I sit here writing at my kitchen table, a ladybird is crawling on my leg. I accidentally bring a lot of wildlife home from work. Beetles and spiders, the occasional grasshopper under my collar, ants in the creases of my work trousers or fallen into my boots.

The ladybird on my knee is trying to unfurl her wings. The red wing cases hinge open and the black, fly-like wings come out – but the right one is broken, bent back, and will not unfold. She tries three, four times, slowly folding it away and then trying to open it again. She wants to leave. Perhaps I damaged her, I don't know. It is easy to damage the quiet fragile things carelessly, to break and maim without even noticing.

Yesterday I was clearing away fallen leaves; a robin hopping behind me was eating the beetles and the worms that I exposed. I uncovered them; they were eaten; the robin ate.

Things break, things scar, and scars are healed, but they twinge from time to time. Every small step we take on this earth has consequences and each evening when I get home I scrub out from under my nails the messy business of birth and sex and death and decay and I try to wash it all away.

It is easier not to think.

I get my hands dirty every day nurturing seeds and pulling up weeds. Playing with chaos, tuning it up slightly to make it a bit more exciting; planting a red garden or a white one; sometimes embracing chaos because we think it is beautiful, and sometimes destroying it because we decide that it is messy. Destroying moles and their apparent chaos is one of the seasonal jobs that comes around every year in a predictable way.

There are intertwining rhythmic cycles that thump along: a weekly mowing of the grass; a yearly pruning of roses; trimming the wisteria three times a year; the annual laurel hedge cut in August; picking apples in the autumn when they tell me they are ready; waiting for the frost before I prune the fruit trees; digging up and storing dahlias after two frosts, then replanting them when the risk of frost has passed. Making compost, planning flower beds, choosing plants and buying seeds in the winter. Planting, weeding and clearing, managing annuals, biennials and perennials, and trapping moles in the winter and the early spring.

The year is marked and celebrated in quarters at the solstices and the equinoxes, and these points mark out the year for anybody involved with nature. They are the beginning points of the seasons. Rhythms, long cycles and short ones, interweave, driven by the ever-changing weather, the duration of daylight and the temperature. Every point is the end of one cycle and the beginning of the next. Each autumn I rake the red leaves from beneath the same maple tree and put them on the same compost heap. Except, of course, they are not quite, not exactly the same leaves, the same tree or the same compost heap as they were last year. The moles I catch in the same tunnels are not the same moles that I caught last year.

These overlapping and intertwined cycles cannot help but take me inside myself to whatever is there on any given day. All I can do is reflect. My wife, Peggy, goes away for her work often, my children are grown and living their independent lives in homes of their own, and I regularly spend days without seeing another human being – two, three, four days in a row sometimes – and am unable to use my words aloud. I have my cat.

I am cold like a spider this morning. It is still very dark. Perhaps I'm too old for this kind of early, but sleep's no longer my lover. I have lost her for ever. She rejects old people like me. The internet says it is because chemical poisons in the environment have calcified my pineal gland. That's how it goes, it says. Mercury, calcium, fluoride. It says I need to eat more chemicals to detoxify. It prescribes yet more turmeric.

My incomplete dreams break into my half-waking life, I'm lost in tunnels alone and chased, I lie there as cold as a frog. I struggle with blocked nostrils (I'm allergic to something indoors), and I watch for a long time while the dark decreases, and seems from blackness to break into fragments, microscopic dots of grey floating, ungraspable, before the dawn, before the sun rises. My muscles hurt and lack strength – I worked all day yesterday and last night I drank whisky. I ponder lifting the covers. I pull myself down into the warmth for just a moment, just a tiny moment. My slow eye transitions from monochrome to colour vision. I think I can see it happen. There is no colour in the world until the daylight comes.

A touch of pink in the grey air and I start to think about coffee, and the thought drives me from my bed. While the coffee hisses into the jug I pick up my cat, who mewls for attention, and we share warmth as I look for a radio station that will give me neither unbearable news nor offensively chirpy music. I've lived through the lives of many cats; I haven't been without one for over thirty years, since Peggy and I have been together. We became a couple and we got a cat. This one, Mimi, is fat and sensuous; she writhes on my lap while I stroke her.

My coffee nearly gone, I feel a little sick; perhaps I am allergic to coffee too. A comedy on Radio 4 Extra about the troubles of a family who have never known fear or hunger.

It is almost properly light now. The dark lasts longer than the light, it is cold, it is December. The breeze is rattling the crisping leaves. I could light a fire and stay inside with Peggy and the cat and watch the day, but I am drawn out as always. I'm not for the indoors, and there is work to do: traps to set, traps to check.

4 a.m.

I woke in a cold dark room
unable to breathe from a bad dream
in which I couldn't breathe

with distance between us
feeling homeless and full of flight
my head beached on the white pillow
like a sand-clogged conch
breath's tide flows in and out
noisily
working through the blocked chambers

drowning

In 2 hours the heating will click on
In 4 hours the sun will start to rise
In 5 hours Peggy will wake up

I look out over the thin winter wood
where buried things will remain buried
until the land is full
and the houses come
and I feel like I am drowning

With a click then a boom
the heating comes on
two quick dark hours gone already
I've been watching the stars
cold and distant yet always there
did I sleep again?
I'm not sure

from a clear starry night the unwanted dawn
crawls across the Rookwood
and beneath the handful of frosted rooftops
in the bare branched wood
the people are waking
and scraping their cars
the rooks perch
and wait for the warming sun
and I struggle to breathe

Peggy stirs
and her head rolls onto my shoulder
heavy and warm
while the scraping continues
and the crows crowd a bare ash

the beetles beetle
and the crows start to crow
and the nearby river
not yet frozen still runs in its flow
while Peggy's stale morning breath
steady and deep
keeps me anchored
with comfort to blanket and pillow

and flow, I think about the flow
and try not to drown

light comes in blinking
and Peggy opens her sticky eyes
and in from chasing woodmice
across the frosted grass
my icy cat curls her cold fur
against my bare feet.

Scything a Meadow

Molecatchers produce advertising flyers and build websites. They tell you that moles on airstrips can cause serious problems for landing aircraft, that the tunnels they dig can cave in under the weight of a galloping horse and riders can be thrown. Horses in paddocks can break a leg by tripping in a collapsing mole tunnel and have to be shot. A handful of moles can cover a vast area of arable land with mole-hills which are quickly covered in weeds, and so crops and yields are reduced, land becomes useless for grazing and farmers suffer financial loss. Moles make more moles, which move to fields next door and spoil yet more crops and grazing.

It used to be that molehills ruined the cutters on the farm machinery used for harvesting grains. Soil from molehills mixed in with grain will spoil it and make it worthless. When this earth is accidentally harvested in animal feed used for silage it can cause listeria in cattle and their milk, and make it unfit for humans. For these reasons farmers have paid out of their profits to employ molecatchers. For hundreds of years, it has made financial sense for them. But things change over time, and farmers are now advised to raise their cutters to avoid many of those problems. Modern machinery is designed to do this, and it works well.

Most gardeners manage a kind of frustrated acceptance of the continual bad weather that can flood a garden for weeks on end. Creatures like rats seem to be universally despised, and will be trapped, poisoned or shot; woodmice are usually enjoyed, hedgehogs are loved. Bee and wasp nests colonising a garden shed and making it out of bounds can be frustrating, but the actions of none of these invaders seem to be taken as personally as those of a mole.

Apparently sane people lose sleep over the chaos the moles create. We do not like to lose control of our property: it makes us feel uncomfortable, impermanent, weak. Moles can ruin domestic lawns, and I have seen real hatred developing in homeowners as they lose control and ownership of their gardens. I have seen people in a temper cursing across the garden. An obsession grows and an endless, unwinnable war can take over their lives.

Moles are tiny, they are cute, and like the rest of nature they do not care what we feel. They are devastating, and they always win. Perhaps some of our anger comes because we like to think of them as being gentle and kind, with an individual personality like Mole in *The Wind in the Willows*, with his big glasses, his good-natured bookishness, his innocence and eagerness to please. Yet in reality the mole is not as introverted and self-effacing as we would like him to be. He takes advantage of us. Maybe we come to think that he is cleverer than we are. Or maybe we have a deeper relationship with and a pride in the things we own and display to others. Ownership of things that appear permanent gives us a sense of permanence. We feel ourselves immortal because of our possessions and the mole coming in and damaging them, taking them away, challenges something buried deep within us.

The effect of his burrowing far outweighs the mole's physical size. When I show a customer a dead mole, many urban gardeners are surprised at how small they are. In the imagination the troublesome mole can grow to gigantic proportions. But usually they don't want to see the dead enemy, just the lawn, the bright shiny lawn, just grass all neat and flat and stripy, under control, safe, for ever.

The mole disrupts the artificial serenity of a lawn in a way that is unacceptable for some. Gardening is not nature: it is using the laws of nature and science to impose our will on a place, and for some people this need for control goes to extremes. I once had a customer with a neat town garden who was obsessed with the branches on his gorgeous magnolia tree being uneven – there were more on one side than the other. No living thing is ever perfectly symmetrical, and imperfection is where beauty is found. But this man counted the branches and cut some of them off to try to make the tree balance. He had no vision of what he wanted, he could only see what he didn't want. I was there setting mole traps when his poor wife returned to see him covered in sawdust, holding his new electric chainsaw, and standing next to little more than a stump. The stump leaned a little to the right.

One of the gardens I work in has a vast flower meadow, and every year I cut this down with a scythe. I use a scythe because it is quiet and doesn't pollute, but mainly because the wildlife has a chance to escape. Brush cutters and strimmers are devastating for wildlife: they slaughter everything in their path. Frogs, toads and hedgehogs are slashed; their flesh is blended into paste. I've done it, and been splashed with blood. Deeply upset at this needless slaughter, I researched alternative ways of cutting down a meadow, and found that I could either invest thousands of pounds in another machine, or I could learn how to use and look after a scythe. I chose the scythe.

The stones in molehills in the meadow take chips out of my scythe blade, which begins every season as sharp as the razor in my bathroom cabinet, but I tolerate them. Every few strokes I stop and hone the carbon steel blade again with a smooth whetstone. At the end of the season I tap out the chipped edge using a peening hammer and anvil, to create a new edge which, like a razor blade, is a single crystal thick.

Scything is a physically hard job that requires plenty of rest breaks, especially as I get older, and so it's a pleasure to stop and put the stone to the blade: it makes a lovely ringing sound when the stone hits the steel, and then a *schwee* sound as it slides along the edge from base to tip, three times usually, alternating from one side of the blade to the other. Then the stone plops back into the water-filled tin holder hanging on my belt and I carry on scything, or just watch the birds for a moment while I get my breath back. Scything too creates a pleasing sound, a long *swishh* with each stroke. It has a good rhythm: swinging from the waist, cutting from the right to the left with relaxed arms outstretched, and striding slowly forward step by step, cutting a swathe up to eight feet wide, and leaving a neat windrow on my left as the stalks fall off the three-foot-long blade. *Swishh*, step, *swishh*, step, *swishh*. Without my even trying, it all ends up co-ordinated with my breathing. *In* as I swing back and step, *out* as I swing for the cut. Long and slow. It used to take me two full summer days to cut down the meadow: now I'm older and it takes me more than three. Next year I may no longer be able to do it at all.

Ahead of me I can often see the small creatures running, shuffling and hopping to escape into the long grass ahead. There's no vicious two-stroke motor screaming and making smoke, so I can hear the hedgehogs rustling and gently move them out of the way. The toads and frogs hop and crawl in front of me and I slow down, or half a dozen field mice rush along and dive into their burrows.

It is a human process, and the tools are simple and brown and honest. I have grown old with these tools: they are handmade of wood, steel and stone, and they have grown old with me and have moulded to my hand. I have a relationship with tools like this: I feel that all the things in the world that I touch are touching me back.

A reaper with a scythe traditionally leaves the last sheaf of grain standing in the middle for the spirit of the crop, 'John Barleycorn', to hide. Then it is bundled and tied and cut with a knife or sickle and taken indoors. I continue this tradition, and bring the bunch of drying wild flowers home.

The meadow is a semi-wild place by a small lake, and we are happy for the moles to live there. They are a part of the ecosystem which includes foxes, field- and woodmice, hedgehogs and millions of flying creatures, including dragonflies, lacewings, hoverflies, pheasants, owls, bats and hawks. The numbers of moles are controlled naturally by the hawks, owls and foxes. Everything here is part of the food chain.

Scything the meadow is done twice a year. In the mid-spring when the grass is growing I cut the new grass back so that the slower-growing wild flowers can come through. Then in late summer, when the flowers have been and gone and shed their seed and the stalks are dry, I cut them down and leave them in windrows on the ground until the sun has dried them and the final seeds have fallen. Most native wild flowers grow best in poor soil, and if I left the stalks

they would rot and increase the soil fertility, so I rake them away in warm, dry weather with a massive wooden hay rake three feet wide and carry them to the compost heap: another day's work.

After the autumn equinox in September, the days become shorter and my telephone starts to ring. People have discovered molehills breaking up the perfection of their lawns and want them to be gone – they make the place untidy. The word 'lawn' comes from the old Welsh word 'Llan', meaning pasture or field. The name of my own village of Llandaff in Wales means 'the field by the river Taff'. This was the language of this island before the Angles, Saxons and Jutes arrived.

My first moles were caught in an immense and rolling country garden in South Wales that I look after, where I am the gardener, but later on I started catching moles in other gardens, too, as it brought me an income in the winter when otherwise I would have none.

In my early days as a gardener I was concerned that the few molecatchers I had come across showed little sensitivity, and that creatures were suffering. Looking back, of course, I have no idea what they felt. I judged them to be brutal men, but I am no different, not any more: the hammer shapes the hand, and I am moulded by the life I chose.

I was aware that the moles were going to be curbed by somebody. I wondered if there were ways other than killing them. I knew that somebody would be called on to do it, and I wondered if that person could be me. So I set about researching and studying the most efficient and humane ways of dealing with moles. I like to learn new skills, especially simple ones that allow me to have a relationship with natural materials, and simple hand tools. I read about the life cycles and habits of moles in books, on websites and in molecatchers' advertising leaflets. I read again and again that the recommended and most humane method of controlling moles was to kill them in traps, and although I looked at all the other options it kept coming back. To get rid of them, you have to kill them.

An old farmer that I met who had been catching moles since he was a child taught me something of what he knew. Leaning on a rickety wooden four-bar fence, wearing his battered hat, he told me how to catch a live mole by creeping along in bare feet while the molehill was moving, and stopping when the mole stopped, and then at the last moment, to pounce on it with a spade and flick it into the air. I have never even tried to do this – I move too slowly. By the time I've got to a mole-hill its maker has usually finished what he was doing and moved on, and my life is too short for me to hurry.

The farmer said that moles like to build permanent tunnels along fence lines, and pointed with one of his massive hands to one such tunnel. This, he told me, had been there since he was a boy, and had been inhabited by generations of moles, one after the other, just as the traditional techniques used to catch them have been handed down through the gener-ations of molecatchers for hundreds of years, one after the other. Farmers are often solitary people, and tend to speak from a distance for a while. The countryside is big, and they are not used to standing close to each other, but once they have started to feel comfortable they like to talk. I usually have a good relationship with them, because I've learned that they have a real and visceral love for the land that they are tied to.

I sat and walked on hillsides and watched the molehills and thought about them, imagined the moles' lives and what they were doing down there. I put my hands into molehills to see what was in them. I tried to work out what kind of pattern the hills made on the surface, and how that might relate to what was going on underground. I wondered why they were on riverbanks and encircled trees, and why they were never in the middle of the playing fields, but were always around the edges.

I wanted to become the best and most humane molecatcher I could, so I bought many varieties of traps. I studied their construction and paid attention to how fast and efficient they were; I tested them by setting them and triggering them with a stick. Some of them were highly technical and would kill a mole quickly, and some simple and brutal traps would just hold the mole in a tight grip until it died, perhaps from blood loss or starvation or cold. I tried to imagine what would happen if a badger or a fox, or a domestic dog or cat, dug the traps up, and I made choices about what kind of trap I wanted to use. Then I started to catch moles. I didn't enjoy killing, so my methods had to be efficient, detached, fast and technical. I had to work to depersonalise the moles, because if, as I believe, all living things have equal value and we are all the same, then I was killing myself. I didn't look at them. I became good at disassociating myself from their deaths.

I used the techniques I had learned, never quite sure if the stories and beliefs were genuine, but I caught all the moles I wanted to catch, and that was enough. I became a very good molecatcher, and word got around. Soon I was getting telephone calls from people who had been given my number by a friend of a friend, and I was getting up on winter mornings to go and meet angry householders who had tried to deal with the mole themselves, and succeeded only in making their lawn worse and training their mole to avoid capture.

I have caught moles in pastures, sports fields, tiny city gardens and immense rolling country estates, and no matter what the land is used for by humans, it is mole territory, and catching them is always the same.

I catch moles for money, and it keeps me busy when the gardens are resting. But of course there are personal reasons that make somebody attracted to this kind of work. When I tell people at parties how I earn my money they laugh. Not that I go to many parties. To people of the towns, understandably, mole-catching is some kind of music-hall joke, something from the colourful rustic past, like being a chimney sweep or a comedic mechanical from *A Midsummer Night's Dream*.

When they stop laughing they become curious and ask lots of questions, mostly about killing things. When I tell them that I have been a vegetarian for fifty years they show me their confused face. Things don't seem to add up. Life is rarely as neat and tidy as we would like. I prefer it that way. Reason is just one of the many important ways of experiencing the world.

When I was young, people would taunt me for being a vegetarian, and call me feeble, weak or squeamish. My younger brothers used to wave meat from their dinner plates at me and say 'Meeeat, it's delicious!' I called them coffin-gobblers, and said I was not a zombie and would rather not eat bits of a corpse. I got slapped across the face for trying to put them off their dinner. None of us changed our minds. We all do what we want to do, and we rationalise it afterwards.

I am old; I have done many things. I went to art school and studied painting and sculpture; I gave it up because I wasn't good enough. My hands are too big and clumsy: they were bred to handle a soldier's rifle, a pickaxe or spade, not a pen or a brush. My body is lumbering and incapable of delicate movement; I am uncoordinated and I make a mess. My handwriting, too, is illegible, but nevertheless my sketchbooks were always full of words. Alongside the scrappy eager drawings of naked women and hopeful flowers and birds were instructions on how to temper steel tools, copied notes about what fire was made of, instructions on how to make a particular shade of blue and why I liked it. There were poems and haiku, but I was at my happiest outdoors swinging an axe, or climbing a hill.

I became a gardener to pay the bills, and to maintain a creative kind of life. When I was homeless I brushed through plants and walked on them, made beds in them, and slept with them against my skin. Woke with green juice on my cheek. I smelled of them. Plucked and chewed on them. How could I spend the rest of my life isolated and not touching their flesh, smelling their infinite palette of individual scents? I began painting with flowers instead of pigment, making and tending gardens. Although poorly paid, there is always work for decent gardeners, and I was determined to learn all that I could.

Naively, when I first began to teach myself about gardening I thought that it would be a nurturing, pastoral and sensual occupation, mostly about flowers, lawns, fruits and trees. I soon learned the pests were part of my job, too. I had to deal with moles, slugs, greenfly, wasps, rats, weeds and many other things that were just getting on with living. For some people much of gardening is about killing things. This has always been an area of conflict for me: my favourite places were the wild ones where I had no killing to do. Killing came hard. But it was either them or me: I had a job to do, a job that I needed in order to feed myself and my family. But killing an insect is one thing, killing a mammal is another. Before I started I wondered what my limits were, what kind of man I was: could I actually do it, and how would I feel when I did?

I was brought up with violence but not with killing. Killing can be, but rarely is, peaceful and kind. Violence is never either. The countryside is full of both. Before molecatching I had never had any need to kill anything deliberately. If there was a fly in the room I would encourage it out of the window. Eventually the time came when I had a real reason to kill something, and I needed to see if I could do it. I tried to focus on killing the moles without doing violence, to do it as humanely as possible.

*

At 7 a.m. I took her tea in her big white mug
she smiled her waking smile from our white bed
slatted with diagonal lines of cold sunlight
I ate porridge, pulled on thick wool socks
and boots and left
driving my van to the red-edged morning sky
through narrow country lanes and to the hills

the invincible planets move on and
creatures stir, and drawn to play my part
as if on a chain with a ring through my nose
I drive the 'A' roads that coil through small towns
    and villages
and tie people's lives together

the dry copper bracken
rolls in redhead waves
to black mountains crushed squat and bowed
under heavy watered blue-black-ink flat cloud
and round a corner slashes of sunlight
flashing off the jagged river far below

then in the dip, autumn's muted shades
distant trees ghostly in dawn's cloud
and the flat-topped flailed leafless hedges
glow pink in the stormy morning sun
as I drive my little van between neat hedges
    singing
into a mist-filled dip then up a hill
and suddenly I'm looking into clear blue sky
and I am not at home any more.

Golden Moles, Star-nosed Moles and Famous Moles

Moles are immensely strong. His massive hands, each of which have two thumbs, are as wide as his head. He has a thick knot of muscle in his neck and shoulders which is as hard as a pebble. I am a working man who lives by the spade and a mole's hands are stronger than mine: a living mole can easily peel my closed fingers apart and escape. The rest of his body is fragile, soft and flexible, so that he can turn around in a tunnel no wider than himself. His nose is wet and pink like a dog's. The mole that I hunt, *Talpa europaea*, the European mole, is as long as my hand and weighs around as much as an empty leather purse. He is covered by dark, blue-black hair that is soft and velvety and brushes just as easily backwards, forwards and sideways, so that the mole can go backwards in the tunnel.

He feels like the best piece of velvet cloth you can imagine. He has whiskers and tiny needle-sharp teeth, so small they look like slivers of glass found sparkling on the kitchen floor days after an accident, which, if I don't catch him, will wear out in a few years as he eats worms filled with sandy soil. There are no visible ears and, if you look carefully by brushing the fur, his eyes can just be seen in the darkness as shiny black dots not much bigger than this full stop. He is a smooth velvet sausage. His back feet and legs are tiny, thin and fragile like a mouse's, and he has a bristly tail an inch long that stands up to feel the roof of his tunnel.

It is said that if you have a purse with a mole's tail attached as a tassel, it will always be full. Moles and magic rituals seem to go well together. It is known among molecatchers that carrying a pair of dried mole hands will prevent rheumatism and protect you from evil; this superstition is found across Europe. Witches love moles as familiars, perhaps because they are dark and secretive. Mole blood and organs can give a person the power of divination if they swallow a fresh, still-beating mole heart (according to Pliny the Elder in his *Naturalis Historia*), and holding a mole in your hands until it dies will give you healing powers. Various mole body parts have the power to cure epilepsy, prevent toothache and ague, control fits and remove warts. Molecatchers of old could make a pretty good extra living by dealing in these 'natural remedies', and were sometimes regarded as 'cunning men', vagrant male witches who appeared when the moles did and left when they were gone, taking their secret knowledge with them.

There are white moles and golden moles in Europe, but they are rare: it is said that if you catch one you will die within the month. I have never caught one. One of the molecatching societies gives you a special badge if you send them a photo of yourself with a white mole. I have the standard gold-plated badge.

In Europe we have just one variety of mole. In Ireland, just as there are no snakes, there are no moles. During the last ice age most of Europe was covered, but as the ice melted about 7,000 years ago the animals moved north following the melt. Many animals did not reach Ireland before the sea levels rose and Ireland became an island.

Across the world there are numerous varieties of mole, most of them similar if not indistinguishable from *Talpa europaea*. North America has seven species: the hairy-tailed mole, eastern mole, broad-footed mole, Townsend's mole, the coast mole, the American shrew mole and the star-nosed mole.

The eastern mole is the most common in the United States, ranging from east of the Rocky Mountains from Michigan all the way down to southern Texas. The hairy-tailed mole, as its name suggests, has a hairy tail unlike the others and is darker in colour.

The shrew mole is the only mole in America that doesn't have large digging hands. He doesn't make molehills; instead he digs shallow surface tunnels in the leaf litter in the rainforests of the Pacific Northwest where he is common. He is the only mole that can put his feet flat on the ground and can climb trees and bushes to look for food. He is often mistaken for a shrew as he is the smallest of the moles, being only four inches long including his long, thin tail.

Townsend's mole is the largest North American mole, reaching nearly ten inches in length including his short tail and weighing up to 5oz. The star-nosed mole lives in wet and swampy areas of North America, foraging for beetles and invertebrates at the bottom of streams and swamps. He is slightly larger than the European mole, and with his massive hands looks very similar, but has a longer, thicker tail. The most obvious difference is the 'star' about half an inch across at the tip of his nose, which he uses to feel his way around and detect his prey. A mole's nose has very specific vibration-sensitive organs, and in the star-nosed mole these have developed into twenty-two pink fingers that look and move very much like a sea anemone: they can detect, catch and eat their prey faster than the human eye can follow. Star-nosed moles build tunnels that often end underwater. The Russian desman is another aquatic mole. He looks very unmole-like: he has webbed feet and a long tail, and lives in family groups in burrows on riverbanks. Again he is blind, has a very mole-like sensitive snout, and is the heaviest of the mole family at up to 18oz and up to 16 inches in length including his tail, which is as long as his body. Due to the desman population's having been decimated by the fur trade, it is now a protected species in Russia.

On a tiny island of Japan called Uotsuri, less than two miles wide, there lives an almost mythical mole known as the Senkaku mole. This mole was first identified in 1979 when scientists visited the island: one of them saw something moving in the grass, hit it with a slipper and took it home. This dead female Senkaku mole is the only one ever recorded, as, due to a conflict between China and Japan about ownership of the island, nobody is allowed to land there.

There are things that look like moles that are not moles, and things that don't look like moles that are – nature repeats itself and uses what it has to fill any gaps. New Zealand famously has no native mammals apart from bats and marine mammals such as porpoises, but Australia has the marsupial mole, which is not an actual mole but certainly looks and behaves like one. It burrows underground in desert areas with massive front hands, is golden in colour, and has a pouch for its young which, uniquely, faces backwards so that it does not fill up with sand. There are other moles that are not moles: mole crickets and mole crabs, the naked mole-rats in East Africa that are insensitive to pain, and all-female populations of mole-salamanders in North America.

You will finds moles throughout our landscape, in our mythology, poetry and literature. Moles, apart from the Russian desman, are solitary animals. Despite this, the delightful Mole in *The Wind in the Willows* becomes friends with Rat, Toad and Badger in this loveliest of all books. Perhaps we cannot help but anthropomorphise the creatures that we do not eat.

In other stories, too, moles appear as far from solitary. Lilygloves in *The Chronicles of Narnia* is a fine gardener and the leader of a warrior group of talking moles. *Duncton Wood*, a romantic story about an ancient empire of moles who worship standing stones in Oxfordshire, is full of battles and escapades. In any number of children's books the mole and his friends have a variety of adventures. Perhaps it is hard for humans to write stories about being alone.

In February 1702 William III, also known as William of Orange, was riding his horse Sorrel in Richmond when Sorrel stumbled on a molehill and threw the king to the ground, where he broke his collarbone with fatal consequences: he succumbed to pneumonia and died the following month. Fourteen years earlier, the Protestant William and his queen, Mary, had deposed the ruling Catholic King James II of England and VII of Scotland. However, many factions in England, Scotland, Ireland and further abroad were supporters of the deposed James, and this gave rise to the Jacobite toast to the mole, 'To the little gentleman in black velvet', which is still occasionally heard today. There is a wonderful bronze statue in St James's Square, London: William, dressed in flowing classical robes, is riding proudly, every inch the victorious king, his horse's head held back and high with flowing mane and, just by his left rear hoof, there is a little molehill.

*

A dawn hillside
looking down into the valley
no pathways or desire lines
I'm walking the field edges
which trace the stream's meander

today's thick frost
could hold a cat's paw
trees and grey sheep still and mute
wait for warmth and light
with dripping leaves and fleeces

the icy air condenses and drips from my moustache
it tastes of snow and rotting leaves
cold air jellies on this old spade's splitting handle
and softens to slush as my hands lose heat
its worn grey T-bar matches
the callouses on my hand
without it I am useless

my body is working
my mind is idling
man-shaped, pig-like
I'm snuffling, bent
I'm leaving booted footprints
in the crystalline grass
and I want to swim
to hang motionless
alone in a loch
my back tattooed with clouds
with seagulls squeaky
wheeling overhead.

Molehills – Leaving Home

It is winter, and bitter cold, and I do not want to leave the warm house, but it is inevitable, unavoidable, inescapable. I have to go to work. The light has at last appeared (darkly) in the Rookwood. My year's work is nearly done. It is cold and frosty, a typical molecatching day.

When I am out in the countryside, walking or hunting, I become solitary and leave my man-nature behind. I become a different kind of creature: something more fluid, free, adaptable and instinctive. This is something that developed in me when I was young and living in the wild. Living moment to moment with no thought or feeling, no ideas or obvious mental process going on, just instinct, an awareness of the field, but not a separate awareness of myself being in the field. We seem to become the same thing. Me, the field, the weather, the scents flowing in and out. Tracking an animal requires this level of awareness, and losing myself like this is an important part of my existence. Not knowing, not thinking, is for me a most desirable state of awareness. Any thoughts I might have seem to be just a reflection upon that awareness, a step away from direct experience that insulates me from the electricity of the moment.

The rusty steel spring latch creaks as I pull on it. It is cold, and the top of the five-bar gate has tiny ice crystals growing in the splitting green wood. It is probably half a century old, and will last at least another fifty years. The gate falls open, driven by its own weight, and it rattles as it hits the earth. I plod through and close it with a metallic clang as the catch strikes. These are the only sounds. Looked at closely, the green cracks in the wood are dark, damp ravines filled with a forest of pine-like lichens where a man could get lost for years. I like to look. Nature repeats itself in all different scales. It leaves a green stain on my hands as I close the gate.

By the gate there are bare willow trees with a small flock of tiny long-tailed birds flicking through the dangling yellow catkins – black and beige, perhaps, a flash of pink or green? They are too fast, and in the dawn under the trees it is too dark to see them properly, but I think I know them. My memory for the names of things is not what it was: it doesn't seem important for me to try and remember. The answer will come of its own accord, or it won't. Words have a different existence to the things they name: they live in different places, have different lives.

In quiet moments like this, there is a sense of completeness: nothing else is needed to make them whole and perfect. I start my work, looking down the field. I go quiet inside; the silence seems to pour out, filling any cracks or flaws in the perfection. Once you experience this feeling of simply existing you lose the need to ask why you exist.

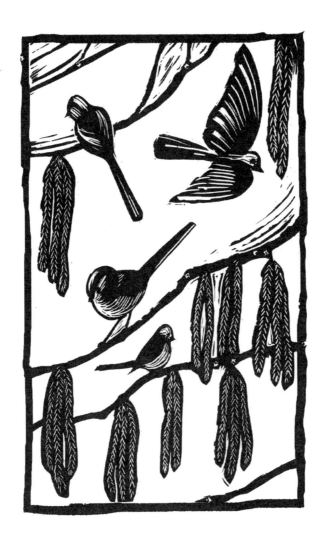

49

Life changes at the solstices and equinoxes. In another winter long ago, the winter of the year I turned sixteen, my mother died, and at the beginning of the following spring my father told me that I was 'surplus to requirements' and should leave. I had no sense of being wanted or being cared about, and so I agreed with him. I packed my rucksack and left early the next morning. I didn't announce it. I didn't leave a note. My few books stayed on the shelf. Family photos, clothes and childhood things still in the drawers. I left my key on the table and closed the door quietly so I wouldn't wake anyone, so I wouldn't have to speak. I am a coward. I left behind all the things that I had accumulated, and I obeyed the call of the void.

I was an apprentice and I earned too little money to rent a place, so I slept out my welcome on friends' parents' sofas, then in derelict houses and an abandoned warehouse. Lying unsleeping through the night on the deck of a half-sunken narrowboat on the Leeds-Liverpool canal, right outside the steel shop where I worked on Wigan Pier, looking up at the stars I decided that I would do what I was good at, which was walking, and that I would do what I enjoyed, which was wandering about and looking at things and trying to figure them out. This was something about me that my father hated. I remember him saying once that I was 'too stupid to come in out of the rain', and thinking, 'But the rain is interesting'. I was a dreamy kid.

I quit my job and started to walk on the towpath. I kept walking for about eighteen months. I left no dust behind, no trails, tried to leave no memories in other people's minds. I like to think I was soon forgotten, passing through like a ghost. I don't know how far I walked because if you are measuring you are not walking. I walked out of town, past the abandoned mill buildings, past the locks and the lock-keeper's cottage, and out into the country, where I remember days when I would sit on my rucksack eating apples and throwing the cores in the slow brown water. Looking at the yellow hazel catkins hanging long and swaying over their reflections. Millions of insects flying low and sometimes dropping down onto the surface, then rising again.

I spent the spring, the summer and the autumn of my sixteenth year walking. The seasons travel at around 2 mph from south to north. If I kept walking north I could have been forever in spring. I think of this as my time of 'sleeping with the birds'. I imagined I was living like a soldier. I walked for miles, avoiding contact with other people. I tried to be invisible. Homeless people are abused, and so I perfected my hiding skills and went underground. Like a mole, avoiding the light, like a worm. Did you know that if a worm is exposed to daylight for more than about an hour it becomes paralysed?

It was a warm spring, luckily, and I had a few pounds saved from my job – a few weeks' pay, a month in hand, a tax rebate and holiday pay. There was nothing that I had to do: no job, no work, no home, nobody to see, no responsibilities. So I walked and watched summer coming slowly to the trees, looking closely at leaf buds tender and sticky to protect their contents from insects. Every so often the canal would pass through a community and I would go into a village shop and buy a few things to eat, and then head back to the path. The towpath was ideal, as there were functioning water taps every now and then for the narrowboat crews which had long since disappeared. Clean fresh water can be hard to find. In the evening, after the dog walkers and anglers and teenage drinkers had left, I had the whole canal to myself. I always took a canal towpath when there was one: a sleeping place is easy to find there; there is no traffic, no noise, no pollution.

At that time nobody used the word 'homeless': people were tramps or 'gentlemen of the road'. 'Homeless' has a different meaning entirely. We used to have a tramp that visited our village from time to time; he had been a soldier, and he stayed in the bus stop just down the road from the pub. Some of the locals would take him a pint of beer, which he drank in the bus shelter where he slept. He never came indoors. He rarely spoke, but he turned up in the summer, stayed for a few weeks, then disappeared again until the next summer. Other people from small country towns I have talked about this to have said, 'We had a man like that too, who came for a few weeks every year and then left.' This happened all over the country. The old molecatchers too lived just like this.

Stone, steel, coal and water
gorse glows across the sheep splotched hills
feet in Welsh mud and head in Welsh sky
this soft light rain
distilled from the sea
and condensed by red sandstone mountains
still seems to taste of salt

I'm in the rotting woods
of damp ferns and spoiled fungus
I could curl and sleep on leaves
where white fat grubs two inches long
eat in the ground

the atheist sees that everything is connected
and that's the true wonder

I'm tired, I'm hungry too and as the sun breaks
    through
and lights the drips on crisping leaves
small birds begin to sing

I've pecked this worn-out year to a stump
and stored its fat for winter
I watched the geese go
I will still be here when they come and go again
my face less smooth
my back less straight.

Earth

Looking down this field, I notice the mole-hills are distributed in groups, sometimes in a relatively straight line, but most of them appear scattered, a Zen puzzle whose distribution is at first sight unreadable, like musical notes without a stave.

I was told by one of the molecatchers who taught me that males go in straight lines and females wander. Gender is fluid, but I'll pass his nonsense on for what it's worth. Living, crawling, swimming, flying things are to me always a 'he' or a 'she' – it would make life easier if I knew a word for a living thing that doesn't fix its gender. I don't like to call living things 'it': that would create an uncomfortable distance between us. I would feel disconnected, alone, disrespectful. The flock of long-tailed tits (I remembered their name) behind in the willows wheel and turn with a speed that makes them appear to be a single fish-like creature – they have a group identity. The flock is an 'it'. Groups are always 'it'. The character of living things changes when they are in groups. I am disconnected from groups; I do not trust them.

In parts of Great Britain and Northern Europe the mole is known as Mouldiwarp or Moldivarp, the earth mover. Moles bring up dark earth from just beneath the surface, turned over, dug to a fine crumb. The kind of damp rich earth that farmers and gardeners love for its texture and nutrients.

Most of the life in the earth is in the top few inches, the place where the moles and the worms and the larvae and the beetles and millions of other organisms do their work. Below this is the subsoil, which is often dense and nutritionally poor, as it has had its nutrients leached away and been compressed under creatures walking and layers of organic matter that has fallen on top. As a gardener I do not dig any more: I hoe off the weeds and top-dress the gardens in the autumn with compost just as nature does with falling leaves and grasses. This keeps the moisture in and the weeds suppressed; it allows the worms to break up hard soil and increases microbial activity, allowing life to expand its range, and lets air and water into the soil. Moles do this for us. Some gardeners still double-dig, but more and more people are coming to understand the importance of microbes and fungi, and often see digging as destructive and prefer to stay off the soil to avoid compacting it.

On the pasture with its pockets of frosted grass, some of the molehills are tiny black humps just about breaking the surface; others are great piles of fresh earth as high as my boot top or more, many crowned with ice. A couple are fresh, made perhaps moments ago, and there are lots of weathered, flattened and weedy mole-hills that have been there a long time. There will have been moles sharing this pasture for generations. I have been here before: the moles keep coming back and so do I. It is mole territory, they will always be here. Molecatchers can only ever control a population. Nature's will to survive is too fierce for men armed only with traps. It takes chemistry to completely destroy a species.

The rolling sloped surface of the earth tells me little about what lies beneath its thin skin, but I have learned to read molehills and know how to imagine the earth below in three dimensions. It has become instinctive to a degree, but there is always more to learn.

The size of a molehill gives me no information about the depth of the tunnel, but its contents and colour give me a clue. Stones or clay from deeper down or light tilth from near the surface – it depends on the structure in any given part of the land.

Moles do not live in molehills; most molehills are just heaps of their household waste, soil and stones, piles of waste that are not visited again unless the tunnel collapses. Often in the molehills there are shards of pottery and glass. In the north of England and Denmark archaeologists sift molehills to look for fragments that moles bring up from underground. They are seeking evidence of previous civilisation without disturbing the site: they call it 'moleology'. Sometimes in molehills I find bits of nylon clothing and baler twine, or the aluminium tops of rusted drinks cans; it depresses me that these un-natural, man-made things refuse to decay and join with the earth. The only permanent things about man are his waste. Natural things decay. There is a bitter-sweet state of existence that all natural things go through, a stage when they stop being what they were and start being something else. I think I am at that point.

Sometimes I see a molehill moving, as the mole inside pushes the earth out of the ground. None of the hills I am looking at are moving: the moles know I am here – they heard me coming from perhaps half a mile away as I wandered down the track with my spade and canvas bag full of traps. There is no other sound here but crows; even the small long-tailed birds are silent.

Moles don't have friends or family; they don't go visiting; they hate company. They do not have a group identity: there is never a gang of moles, never an 'it'; no collective noun is ever used because they are never together, unless they are dead. Then you can choose your own noun if you like: heap, pile, stack, bucket, bag, row, etc.

The world of the mole and me is one where there are no crowds to either rise above or be outside of, to be part of or to avoid. In their world and mine there are a few related individuals and their networks. A world mostly devoid of others, but the machines are coming and the houses and the people: we are close to the city and transport links. Not to this field, not just yet, but I drive past the yellow machines every day as the city creeps further and further out into the countryside.

Although moles avoid each other I can see that there will be several moles in this field, each with their own possibly overlapping territories. De-focusing my eyes and withholding any judgement I look for patterns and distances between each scattering, and this helps me to see roughly how many moles there may be. I estimate that this small field that I can gently walk around in about forty minutes could support a population of about a dozen moles. I squint down the acres and count, maybe ten or twelve different territories, some overlapping each other.

There is a river on my right – the earth on that side of the field is stony and grey and has lots of clay. An otter has left footprints in the mud bank, and kingfishers, cormorants, herons, swans and various ducks have returned since the mines closed miles upstream. In the summer the unemployed miners and their children sit on the banks up there with fishing rods. There are salmon and trout. The people have been devastated; nature has flourished. A few of the men have become homeless but remain, resisting the suction that draws many south. Others have gone, leaving boarded-up houses, dead homes, thirty miles up the river where there is no work. Rows of small houses tucked quiet on hillsides in the valleys. In the summer homeless people from near and far sometimes sleep downstream, hidden in the scrub on the riverbanks, some of them in tents. In the winter they go into town where there is shelter from the wind. Some stay around, some move on, some die.

This is the river Taff, that starts high in the Brecon Beacons where I like to walk and sleep out sometimes. Fifty miles later it flows through the middle of Cardiff, past the castle and the rugby stadium and into Cardiff Bay. This piece of land I am working on has been pasture for centuries, and is deep and black. Here I am myself, an animal like the others: I have no behaviour that I must explain, nobody to explain it to. I am here to catch the moles. The simplicity of being here in this solitary task leads me deeper and deeper into that magnificent connectedness that gives me what I need. A heron, almost invisible, waits for small fish in the tangle of tree trunks left from the storms, hanging on for a flood to send them out to the sea. A cormorant floats by.

I have a habit of coming back to these places. I have enjoyed having a territory of my own: there is a freedom in having a regular place to return to – it takes away the need to think about it and allows a person to rest. A sense of belonging was something that I wanted to give to my children, but I also have an unease about having a specific place to belong to. A feeling of belonging brings with it a desire to build something to mark one's connection, and then, having built – a garden, a house, a career, a tunnel system – one has to protect those things from intruders, violently if necessary. We try to create an illusion of permanence, but there is none.

I lived an early life that involved a lot of travelling from place to place. My family were always on the move, relationships with people and places always short. Friendships, impossible to sustain, never lasted beyond the honeymoon period, always intense. I was born a long way from where I am now. I have a culture which came from my parents and grandparents and the people I grew up around. They gave me fragments that they passed on from their parents. Things distantly related to different parts of this land. Mannerisms, tastes, habits and tics passed on from great- and great-great-grandparents that I never could have known. People who are no more than ghosts appear in my behaviour. That is all that I have: no photographs, no heirlooms. I do not have a land.

I have wandered around much of this island and slept in it. I feel it is all mine, it is all everybody's. I was born to vagrants, my grandparents Scottish, Irish, Manx and Lancastrian. Soldiers, railwaymen and mill girls who travelled to find employment or escape from poverty, or just because they were bored. Before the Industrial Revolution they would have been itinerant farm workers, perhaps even molecatchers. Only one grandfather lived his whole life in the Lancashire town where he was born, and he had a Welsh surname. Perhaps I have come home.

I once knew an Irish family who called themselves gypsies. They lived in a house in the city and talked often of the difficulties they had trying to live next door to country people. When I asked what they meant by 'country people', they told me it was their name for people who belonged to a country.

Home is a place that we are supposed to love and respect; it gives us a sense of loyalty. Without a home we do not have that loyalty, that sense of nationality. Here in South Wales I feel as 'at home' as I have ever felt anywhere.

I created a home where I ended up. A place that feels good, where I made a nest with my wife and we made children. I chose a place to live, we all settled in. It is a territory that has become familiar, and that makes it easy to navigate and survive.

In the north of England and Scotland they do not ask where you live, or where you come from: they ask, 'Where do you stay?' as if living somewhere were just a stop on a journey, as if we were all travellers. Here in Wales is where I decided to stay. It is the dip in the bed that I roll down into when I am tired, the place where my woman and my children know to start looking for me. But in reality, we are all travellers.

My sense of identity came not from any place where I have lived, but arrived when I became a gardener, and realised that my home was simply the outside, the countryside, wherever it was. When I step off the carpet or the floorboards and onto the ground, I know who I am. I belong on the earth and I love the soil. It's a living organism, and I want it on my skin. It makes me feel good to walk, barefoot if possible, barehanded, bareheaded, my body connecting the air to the earth. It's the final place of all that lives and grows. The feeding place of everything. The nature of my life has become the nature of the rocks and the trees and the muddy water and the rain that falls in it. These things consume me, and to live as if they were not there is unthinkable.

I work as a gardener in mown and tended places that are used to entertain and impress, but my heart is not there: it is in the woodlands and meadows, the wild places where ferns grow in damp shade, rooted in fallen trees. Places where streams are overhung with foxgloves or willow, dark springs and ponds where leaves fall and rot and bubble deliciously like the earth's cauldron. These were the places where I used to wander as a teenager and sit for hours and make my bed, these are the places where I feel safe.

Eating the apples that nobody picked
half a dozen blackbirds or more
they know nothing
they make no plans for the future
yet they prepare for winter

toad flops by while I kneel
and we are equal
and I fall in love again
a solitary heathen

running water meeting rock makes
sparks run up my spine
I am exposed
I can never return from here

pines dark green reach high and swing
against a sky – ice blue and clear
and in their shade there's frost
and shelter
I imagine a bivvy for the night
and waking glittering cold
making morning tea
on a smoky twig fire

I am a stag

I am a fox

I am a carp

I am a rook

I am a naked forked animal wrapped in wool

with mud on my hands.

Tunnels and Sleeping

I am tired. It is cold and I would rather be at home now and still in bed but there is work to be done so I'm wrapped up in wool and cotton layers and making steam. This small field looks like a battleground: the once grassed surface is now mostly molehills and mud. It is a field owned by the archery club, and it looks as if it has been bombed. There is a long tradition of archery in Wales: Welsh bowmen were much prized on the battlefields of England and France.

The field is on a hillside where the edge of town becomes country: there's a small housing estate five minutes' walk in one direction, and the fields in the other direction spread as far as the next town. One town or another will eventually absorb it, I suppose, and the moles will then pop up in somebody's garden instead. Behind a wire fence on the left there is a railway line raised up on ballast, and a tanker train thunders past. The driver blows his two-tone horn. The moles don't mind.

On my right the bank falls away through scrubby land infested with Himalayan balsam to the river. On the other side of the river there are more fields and tree-topped hills spreading into the distance. The bottom of the field has been left to turn into woodland, mostly deciduous wild trees bare of leaves now. Ash, hazel, willow, a couple of holly trees. Trees that have self-seeded. I know their names. They are trees that I have used for fuel.

Behind me the farm gate is part of an overgrown hedge, with a little coppice off to the left. It is no longer a hedge: it is gappy enough to walk through. I used to look for such places to sleep in. There is leaf litter, shelter from wind, space to stretch out. You can tell that the hedge was laid many years ago because the older, thicker stems are horizontal, pointing left, and then branches grow out of them, shoot upward, become trees. Ash, blackthorn and hawthorn. I would guess from the thickness of the stems that the hedge was last laid maybe fifty or more years ago. Down the track to the field somebody has started to lay another hedge. It is rare to see this in this area now: obviously somebody is learning the craft. I have learned some of these skills myself over the years – drystone walling, hedge-laying – but they need a lot of labour and no longer make economic sense. These skills are disappearing, and it is only the passion of our farmers that keeps our remaining hedges and stone walls maintained. Drystone walls were a major habitat for toads, snakes and lizards, and so these too are now dying out.

I wash my hands with soil from a molehill to hide my scent. I pull a piece of broken pottery out of the molehill, turn it around, take a liking to it and put it in my pocket. This handful of soil like all good soil is a mixture of sand, rotting leaves, twigs and bits of insect and mollusc shell. Each handful teems with the life of beetles, worms, billions of microscopic bugs, nematodes, slimes, bacteria and fungus, which eat the rotting vegetation and each other. Slowly the ever-reducing particles pass through one tiny organism and then into and through another smaller one, mixing in with their gut bacteria that break down the plant and animal waste which the earth is made of into its constituent minerals, so that tiny micorrhizal fungi living on the fine roots of plants can absorb them and transfer them into the plant roots, in a symbiotic relationship which only now is becoming fully understood. Pull the leaf litter away in a woodland area, just to a depth the thickness of your hand. Before you see it you will smell the mushroom scent of the mycelium. The earth's intestines. This enormous network of white threads collects minerals and rotting organic plants and animals. It connects every growing thing together, wrapping around the microscopic hair-like plant roots, passing on nutrients and allowing the plants to take in the minerals and chemicals they need. These organisms and their intimate interconnec- tions form the digestive system of the living Earth of which we are part.

My hands are covered with this living brown earth and a billion microbes. Both inside and out I am part of this vast living and dying, constantly cycling organism that spins and mixes, rinses and dries its decaying parts like clothes in a washing machine. Without these organisms living on, in and outside our bodies we cannot survive.

Not long ago I watched a camera travel through my intestines. It wandered through my tunnels, showing them pink and juicy on the screen, hunting for cells that should not have been there and zapping them with a hot wire loop. I was struck by the similarity between the bacteria that inhabit the soil, and those which inhabit my gut. Mycelium and intestines and bacteria breaking down nutrients so that cells can absorb them. When I got home I researched these gut bacteria and how to feed them, and now I pamper them as if they were my tiny pets. I cannot break the feeling that all I am is a network of transport tunnels, an alimentary canal with a support system that allows it to move around so that it can feed and reproduce.

So much of what happens depends on unknowable mysteries that work away, hidden beneath the surface. In the earth a mole is part of the earth's own digestive process. He eats the worms that eat the leaves that they pull down into their own tiny burrows. The mole leaves his clues about his activity written on the ground in a language that tells a vague and untrustworthy story about where he is and how deep he is. He is rarely seen. Reading his story, decoding his secrets, finding him and sending him back to the earth before his time, to be recycled by the slugs, grubs, beetles and worms that he would have eaten, is my solitary and almost silent job.

A mole can dig about 20 metres of tunnel in a day, packing soil into the roof and walls with his big hands as he goes. He also pushes soil ahead, and eventually there is too much to push. He makes a diversion and pushes the earth out onto the surface. Sometimes I catch sight of him briefly sticking his giant pink hands out of a molehill.

Moles will dig under walls, paths and boundaries, they will swim rivers and streams, and tunnel under foundations. In his three-dimensional world, the mole goes up and down, twists and turns to avoid rocks and roots in search of food. Feeding tunnels take a meandering route: they may intersect and cross one another and divide off in different directions.

How deep he digs his tunnel often depends on the weather and the type and depth of soil. I have heard stories of moles going deep, of a sexton seeing a mole run across the bottom of an empty grave – it's a story that I have heard several times, but never from anyone who has actually seen it. The world runs on fiction.

Moles have at least two kinds of tunnels: feeding tunnels which twist and change direction, and permanent tunnels which often run along field boundaries, along the base of walls, and under fence lines and hedges where moisture drips and soil remains damp and undisturbed. Permanent tunnels are often quite deep, and make up the backbone of the mole's system: this is his home. If there is plenty of food he will just patrol these tunnels looking for worms and beetles that have fallen in. In times of food shortage he will expand his network, dig feeding tunnels, and new molehills will appear.

Some tunnels are shallow, and raise the grass in tight meandering curls of turf which just appear from nowhere on the surface. One of the old molecatchers that taught me called it 'running wild': he said that the mole, driven crazy by hormones, was looking for a mate. I have no idea why he thought this – perhaps it said more about his lonely life than that of the mole. I think the mole might have just come across a group of worms or beetles who had found a bunch of nematodes or a rotting leaf to eat. Everybody has an idea, but nobody knows. We don't need to know everything to catch them; being comfortable with not knowing is an important part of hunting, as it keeps all the options open, offers choices. Not knowing is for me the best of all possible worlds; it contains a sweetness and a playful willingness to accept change and to enjoy the multi-layered, million-petalled flower of life without having the compulsion to know what everything is. These surface tunnels seem to be rarely used more than once, and when I see them I just press them down. They do no harm to the land, and they don't pop up again.

If you look carefully in woodland, you will often see around the tree a ring of molehills, old and new; this is where the moisture drips off the leaves, which causes the leaves to rot, and the beetles and the worms to gather, and the mole to dig his tunnels. Possibly he'll spend the rest of his life just going round and round hoovering up the food that falls out of the tunnel walls, like a Tube train on the Circle line. Occasionally he might dig side tunnels, branch lines, but he'll always return to the main line.

When I visit the capital and travel on the Tube sometimes I imagine that I am a mole going around his tunnels, switching from one to another in the darkness, hunting and stopping from time to time. At other times I am a miner heading for the coal face. Like many others, I suspect, I have a love/hate relationship with the Tube. Either way, unlike the mole, I can't wait to escape and reach the surface. I do not feel at home under the ground. But the mole only ever leaves his tunnels to mate, and every time he will return. His predictability, his need for a permanent territory, and his aversion to change, are the weaknesses that will lead to his being caught.

I start my hunt by finding the most recent hills, the ones made in the last few hours, unflattened by foot, hoof, rain or wind, with crumbly, moist, unweathered earth freshly brought up from beneath the surface. This tells me where he is working at the moment. He will travel between these fresh workings and his main permanent tunnel, so I will be looking to trap him somewhere between them.

The leaves fallen just a few months ago are starting to turn into soil already. There are snowdrops sprouting in clumps where somebody must have planted them at the base of an oak tree, and I wonder why they did that in this bare field. A tribute? A votive offering? Even the wild places show the hand of man.

There is pain in my joints and muscles. I have to accept that I am getting old and will not always be able to carry this heavy bag of traps or endure this cold. Perhaps the time is nearly here for me to move on. I prefer to stop and look rather than to work. I remind myself that this is a part of life that I have been looking forward to, but seeing those snowdrops on a breezy cold hillside just triggered these thoughts. I cannot choose to stay the same; change is all there is – it just happens. A shell of ice in a tractor rut creaks as I step on it, crows creaking in the bald, windblown, creaking trees. Creaking knees.

I walk toward the river to do a circuit of the field boundaries where the main tunnels are likely to be, trying to figure out the movements of the moles. Down the field by the river which, even now, so close to freezing, still smells of river. There are always smells. Across the bottom under the trees and then back up by the fence. The path a molecatcher walks is always coiling, and like a labyrinth eventually ends up in the middle. And there, of course, is only peace and quiet, and the simple perfection of things being just and only what they are.

As I walk around the field I can't help noticing the odd place, under a massive rhododendron for instance, that might make a safe and sheltered bed for the night – a habit of looking that I have never broken. I notice potential overnight stops as a matter of course, wherever I am. To be able to rest is perhaps the most important physical and mental survival skill that I have. Tiredness is lethal. The most restful place I know is under a tree – any tree other than a holly – on a warm spring evening, watching the webs drift across the branches and waiting for the blackbird to sing me to sleep as the stars begin to show through the darkness.

Evergreens make good shelter, as they shed their leaves all year round and provide bedding that smells clean – and because the leaves are resinous they tend to rot slowly, and stay dry until they are well buried under a new layer. Decay creates its own heat, as organisms are converted into chemicals and minerals. As the buried layers decay, they warm up and dry out the top layers. Deciduous trees shed leaves only in the autumn or in times of drought, and their leaves attract moisture: they want to rot. Large bushes are good places for a man to build a nest for the night. Pine forests are better.

When I was sleeping with the birds I felt that I was the same as the wild animals I slept with;

we were engaged in the same activities for the same reasons. We were all just going about our business. I slept under hedges, on riverbanks and beaches. I would fall asleep listening to the waves bringing tiny stones rattling up onto the shore and the water bubbling back down through them, or the river falling through the rocks while the owls hooted to each other from the forest, or listening to the torrents pouring from the sluices in a lock gate and looking at the clouds rushing over the abandoned red-brick cotton mills and reflecting in the thousands of broken window shards remaining in the corners of their rusting iron frames.

Often at night I would hear a blackbird. The blackbird is a sentinel bird: it picks a vantage point at the top of a tree and sings its sweet and complex song as it looks out, but when it sees danger – a cat or a crow or hawk or a man – it sends out an alarm call warning all the birds and other creatures around. At the day's end I would settle and stop and become still and quiet, and the blackbird who had watched me come would change its call from an alarming *scree* and *chink chink chink* and relax as I did, and begin to sing its complex, mellow song again until, as darkness fell, it would utter one last call and fly off to roost in the bushes, just like me.

The more silent I was, the more I could hear. The animals relaxed: they knew that I was there but was no threat. The more noise I made, the quieter nature became. Keeping still, I would understand what was around me. In the dark I could feel the cold, damp air of a body of water, or the silence of a managed pine forest where there's shelter and safety but little wildlife, or I could listen to the noise of an old woodland, where every inch of surface is populated by something that chirps or runs, flies, jumps, crawls or slides, or just sits and absorbs moisture. The physical weight of an approaching storm.

In the dark I could listen, smell and even feel with my skin much farther than I could see. I never thought to get a torch: a torch would mean batteries, and every penny was needed for food. I remember one night leaning against a tree at the edge of a field and jumping from rest into a high, adrenaline-fuelled alert in the pitch-black, listening to somebody coughing in the field right next to me. It went on all night, and I stayed stock-still for hours. In the slow dawn I learned that coughing sheep sound exactly like humans. Another night, as I was drifting off, a rustling from the hedge I was lying by, then occasional footsteps and heavy breathing, turned out to be a horse dozing on the other side.

If you are not too fussy there is always somewhere to sleep on a riverbank or canal bank, or by a field. I learned to make myself comfortable. Where hedges were well tended and banked and ditched they did their job and kept me out. Older, untended, gappy hedges provide mature trees, and there are often ideal resting places just behind them. Such hedges are usually the remains of ancient woodland that has been cleared for agriculture. Trees provide privacy and shelter from wind and rain if they are thick enough. Sometimes they are in double rows, with a gap in between them where a comfortable camp can be made for the night. Down in a ditch the night hangs longer, and I could sleep tight for as long as I liked.

The only animals I fear are cows, dogs and people. Wild animals leave you alone. I have woken with frogs and snails on me and all kinds of insects, but have only ever been bitten by insects and stung by wasps and bees because of my own carelessness.

Sleep usually came quickly after a day walking, and was the length of the darkness. In the spring and autumn the night was long, and in the summer sleep was short. I would settle down at the same time as the birds and watch the sun set over the water or the hills to the west, and wait for the dawn. Then, later, wake with the birds: first the blackbird, then the robins, as the sun rose behind me and lit up the mist or the dew on the grass and leaves. As I lay there I had an idea that there might be omens. That if I saw a magpie it might mean that I would get something nice to eat that day. That three crows might mean a change was coming. I was too young to know that change is always coming, and it doesn't announce itself.

At night, when I rested, I dissolved into the earth and the night as if I was made of them. I was not in nature: I didn't 'commune' with it – I was nature, as close to my true nature as it was possible to be each day, all day, every day. And every morning leaving my bed at dawn with perhaps the briefest backward glance, never to return, never to own it or have that same experience again, that bed, that view. These places were, and still are, my home.

Above me the sun and the moon
and endless cycles
from solstice to equinox and round
which tell me when to work
and when to rest

the days are short
this one's bright
but I am feeling old and dull
and working makes my day feel long

cold wet wind and sky flow in
and I taste it on its journey to my lungs and out
the sheep here breathed it first
we'll share some molecules
at the edge of this winter forest

at the edge
that makes me a thing with horns
at the edge of this rain
at the edge of this short dark day
of damp leaves and wet places
at the edge of living and not
where hedgehogs rustle
and things rot

and fungus thrives
and my shadow shortens
and week becomes month
becomes year
becomes life
at the edge I remember to remember
to have compassion
and I feel connected again

the changing seasons change everything
everything cancels out everything else
the sound of everything at once is silence
the colour of every colour at once is white.

Getting Old and Walking

Moles live only in their territory, and they know it well: they can remember their way in the underground blackness and they travel at speed. They seem to feed in different parts of their system in rotation, first clearing their prey from one area, then moving on for a day or so. They are slick and quick. Changes in the tunnel made by a trapper or a creature breaking in will scare them, and they will block it up and move to a different part of the same system, building new tunnels and making new hills. Weasels and stoats will dig into the tunnels and hunt them down, and the mole will flee, backfilling the tunnel as he goes.

If a mole comes face to face with another mole outside of the mating season and does not turn back, they will fight to defend the tunnel until one of them is mortally injured and goes off to die. Fighting is in the nature of things with territories. The mole will most likely die of internal injuries, because his blood has very little ability to clot – they bleed to death from even the slightest injury. Occasionally mole tunnels will break into each other, and in adjoining tunnel systems they call to each other by twittering to make sure they do not have to meet, like cyclists on the towpath to work, ringing their bells to avoid an accident.

Throughout the summer there could be any number of moles living quite happily underneath the garden without anybody knowing, but as the weather turns colder and the worms go deeper, food becomes harder to find, and they start to expand their territories, and this is when I get called out, as hills appear where there were none before.

Adult moles rarely adventure about on the surface. Out of their tunnels, on the surface, they are slow, juicy and vulnerable, and they will be eaten quickly. Where there are moles there are often crows and other birds waiting for them to drive worms up to the surface, but the crows and birds of prey will take a mole if they get the chance. Domestic cats and foxes will also wait stealthily by moving molehills and pounce as the mole shows his hands.

Most moles will travel on the surface only when they leave the nest in the spring as young. They wander a sufficient distance from their home and then dig and start a tunnel system of their own, or if they are lucky they find an abandoned one. Nobody knows how they know when they are far enough away. How does any creature choose his territory? My supposition is that they use their sense of smell, and when the smell of home fades and there is no smell of other moles they start to dig. They have never dug before, and either they do it by instinct or in a bid to escape predation. In times of drought I have heard of moles being found on the grass where the soil is shallow and the earth is dry; they are looking for water or food perhaps, and apparently they sometimes travel overland during the breeding season, but I have never seen it. My territory, around South Wales and the Vale of Glamorgan, is mostly rich, deep farmland, and the moles stay underground.

There is no night or day in the darkness underground. Moles seem to have a four-hour cycle, feeding for four hours, then sleeping for four hours, in one of several nests in the tunnel system. Molehills appear overnight in gardens because they are often quietest then, but in peaceful land they can pop up at any time.

Moles are small and powerful, vicious subterranean predators. I have read that they need to eat more than half of their bodyweight every day, and will eat up to 20kg of worms a year.

Moles are virtually blind. European moles can see light and dark, but not much else: they cannot focus. Others, such as the Russian desman, are totally blind. Moles will walk right over a dead worm, but will track down a living, moving one from some distance away, pulling them from the tunnel walls or picking them off the tunnel floor and eating them head first, pulling them between their fingers like a climber on a rope as they eat.

Moles go where the worms go, and when the weather drives the worms deep, the moles go deep. Even the heaviest rain doesn't penetrate deep soil unless it is in a valley and the land floods, or there are plenty of trees. Rain runs off the surface and is drained away by tunnels close to the surface: like the trees, they are part of the way that nature prevents flooding and soil erosion. Although moles can swim well with their big hands, they can drown in flooded tunnels, as can worms. Moles, or the worms they hunt, may be sensitive to air pressure. I have sat on a hillside for a day or so and watched new molehills being thrown up further uphill when the air pressure drops and rain is coming.

The frost penetrates even less deeply than the rain, no more than a few inches. In cold weather the moles carry on as normal, often breaking through frost or snow to leave a mound of rich black soil on the surface. They don't hibernate. Underground it is always warm.

When drought dries the earth out, the worms go deeper to find the moisture that they need, and obviously the moles will follow them. But if the soil is shallow over rock, and drought comes, the worms die. When there is no organic matter being created or recycled, the soil blows or washes away when the rains arrive, leaving bare rock. Shallow soil needs the trees to bind it together and raise the moisture levels, and to drop leaves and bring life. If the soil washes away, the rock will be exposed and on the rocks lichens will grow that will adapt to the falling oxygen levels and rising CO_2 and temperatures and rainfall. There will always be a life of some kind and there is no point hanging on to anything, anything at all. This ceaseless gyre of wind and water on rock and flesh makes them all one. There is no otherness.

The hedgehogs, toads and frogs that I shared my leaf litter with when I was a wandering boy are slowly disappearing because of pesticides, and their fields and woodlands are being turned into houses and roads. I accept the new conditions, I have become used to them. I have learned to live with the constant rain, the lack of winter or summer, the roses blooming in December. It all just becomes normal.

Damage is part of the flow of things. I am growing older and my body continues to dissolve. Under the flesh of my wrist I can see my beating tide. My own loose spring pulsing underneath a spiral where a tattoo needle scratched some curling grooves.

My heart beats its own rhythm, which breaks and speeds and slows sometimes, and stops and starts and I breathe in 'squares': in for five beats; hold for five beats; out for five beats; hold for five beats to control my heart rate, or at least cope with it. I am a ticking clock winding down. I eat pills to thin my blood and avoid the clot that may one day stop me from knowing who I am, who Peggy is, who my children are. I cannot smell things any more. 'Sans eyes, sans taste...' My eyes are losing their sharpness. That is how it goes.

I used to be able to hear bats. There is a perpetual stereophonic scream of dying receptor cells in my ears which if I resist is unbearable, but if I accept it I can tune in and listen and play with it. Tinnitus. This howl I experience as real, but it is not real: I can hear it yet nobody else can. No sensitive listening machine can pick it up; it is immeasurable yet its truth is in the experience, like the taste of a smoky, salty glass of whisky. Truth is only ever in the experience. I can hear the ghosts of whale song and trains passing and arrows in flight. I am told by audiologists that the sounds are always there, but if I focus on something else they go away. If I fix my gaze on a leaf just hanging on and waiting to drop, and I wait to catch the moment when it leaves the tree, an hour can go by in utter silence.

I rarely hear small birdsong any more. I can see the tiny beaks opening and closing like mussels in a rock pool, like lobster claws or barnacles silent in the thickness of water, like daisies at dusk. There should at least be clacking. My daughter's voice fades in and out; my high frequencies are gone. Sometimes in the quiet of the night there are other sounds and I ask Peggy if she can hear them too. We talk constantly about our daily lives and concerns. In so many ways we need each other to be able to know what is real and what isn't.

My mind is losing its need to control the world around me too: I let things be what they are; I am a lotus-eater. I forget easily and willingly, and because of this Peggy and I rarely argue, each day begins with a forgiveness for things that may or may not have happened. Eventually my mind may lose its need to control my body. I have made my children; nature does not need me any more. These are my unavoidable personal ecologies. You have your own, but they will be similar. Healing is just adapting to change, acceptance. It is all normal, we come in and grow, then fade back out again.

I have grown to love this ground that I walk on, the rain, the mud, the birds and mammals and even the insects that bite me in the summer, the butterflies, hoverflies, dragonflies, crowds of wasps and bees, grass and trees, and the moles that I know and track and hunt, whose bodies I hang on the fence or throw to the birds or return dead to their tunnels. The buzzing vibrating energy that expresses life and its cycles. I feel a physical excitement when I step out of my van with my bag and put a foot on the wet green earth that is almost sexual.

The hot summer days were long and tiring and I wouldn't walk far: I would seek shade and water. In warm weather, dog walkers and anglers would be out on the towpaths and riverbanks. I didn't walk hard, this was not a sport, I sauntered, *sans terre*. I could sit under a tree unseen, ignored until darkness came and they all drifted away like dandelion seeds on the breeze, and I was alone again and perhaps would walk a little in the cooler air.

Hills in the distance always appear whiter than those that are closer. In the distance they are white against the white sky and almost invisible. At their limits, when things and people are almost nothing, they are at their most delicate. If I were to walk backwards I could watch the hills fade and be gone back into cloud. As I approached they became darker and more solid, and new white hills appeared behind them. Slowly, hour by hour or day by day, I got to know the darkening hills well in all the shades of daylight and weather, and from different angles as the path turned, climbed and fell.

I had no plan, no goal, other than to walk and be outside. I wasn't trying to get anywhere, there wasn't anywhere to be. No time limit, nothing to achieve. There were just the footsteps, the day, the second, one breath after the other, the gently swinging door. There came a joyful freedom in watching the world all day long with no responsibilities other than to eat from time to time, and to find a place to rest when it got dark.

At some point on a long walk you stop being who you thought you were, but you don't question it because the questions stop too. I became for a while just steps and breathing. Walking and resting. Everything fell away: all the small nonsenses of life that had seemed so large. My identity destroyed. My individuality killed as I became one with everything. Walking for a long time dissolved all of my negative and positive feelings about myself and about others. I became completely empty: there were no anchors, nothing at all to hang on to. What was left was just acceptance and love of what is. Anything else just seemed ridiculous. The 'self' that I learned through childhood to present to the world was lost, and I have left it behind now for long enough that it has become impossible to construct any kind of solid immutable 'self', because I don't know how to do it. I am always aware from moment to moment that behind the mask there is nothing, and that very silence is the most wonderful, the most perfect, thing there is.

I flowed like a river around obstacles, sped up and slowed down depending on the landscape and the temperature. Sometimes I got trapped in eddies and stayed in the same place for a couple of days. There were rarely any thoughts of being in another place, so there was no hurrying. Five or ten hours of walking was five or ten full hours of taking each step one at a time, breathing and seeing and hearing the wild things or the wind or the rivers that wind through the woods that reach into the air that flows in and out and in, to blood and pumping heart and muscles that move me along and through it. After a week or two I became just a movement in the air. The sound of a falling stone on the path.

At some point I left the towpath, but I have no memory of where. As time passes, memory inevitably consumes, recycles and recreates itself: I was a boy and now I am old. I walked country lanes and abandoned railway lines and riverside paths. Fragmented memories of crab-apple trees and hawthorn heavy with newly opened blossom that brought the wind that took the blossom away. Walking through the seasons from daffodils to bluebells, then massed dandelions turning from bright yellow heads into white clouds of seed drifting across the path so thickly it was hard to breathe. Then as the days grew longer and warmer, and walking was harder, I saw ox-eye daisies sparring alongside last year's teasels, which were still standing brown and dry. I watched the cow parsley and wild carrot appear from clenched green fists and grow to great frothy white heads with bees and hoverflies and other flying insects buzzing around them, and the millions of foxgloves fade in the heat, and the buttercups that were scattered through the long grass. I walked past ferns as they turned from tiny curling croziers into great fronds that slowly turned brown and died, leaving little buds of next year's croziers curled tight against the coming winter. I passed dog roses while they turned from red rosehips to small pink flowers, and back to green rosehips.

Hedgerows are some of the most truly wild places, where things are allowed to blossom and bees and other insects pollinate and birds nest. Long, thin, wild places that mimic the woodland's edge. The wonderful scent of wild garlic at a wood's edge that tempted me to risk a nibble, then wait for signs of poisoning. Later in the year, black-berries and the odd apple. I was surrounded by plants that I could have eaten: some of them delicious, that could have made my life a little easier, some of them that would have killed me in hours. But I did not know about either until much later, when I found a home and had a place to collect and store books to learn from, and started to get lost in the wilderness for fun.

I saw rooks and jackdaws in their hundreds foraging, all facing south, strutting along pecking at the ground like chickens. I saw hawks circle and stoop and dive, and I learned that there are birds of the sky, birds of the trees, birds of the low shrubs and birds of the ground. I saw blackbirds that sing at the treetops in the darkness of morning and evening, that nested in shrubs at night and fed on the ground in the daytime. Robins nesting and feeding in low trees. Tiny flocking birds that flit from shrub to shrub. I saw birds learning to fly. I saw and was watched by owls and wood pigeons. I saw lambs born and newborn creatures die: a newborn lamb attacked by crows, birds fallen from nests, dead sheep in a clearing that I smelled from half a mile away, a dying fox under a tree. Roadkill by the ton. I learned that animals in the wild do not die of old age comfortably in their beds.

Old on an old hill alone
walking bent at the edge of the woods
of old bent oak and hawthorn
steam from the mossy branches
as the low sun hits

I only ever walk single steps
thousands and thousands of them
one after the other
each one their own separate thing
looking down

long strands of web drift and wrap
around me, a tiny spider in my beard
I want to starfish on the mown meadow grass
have the birds and multitudes of insects
take me away cocooned in silk
to the cold cloudless heartless sky
before the bone-white winter
begins for all
the end for some

I am oak and strong
but wood becomes mud
and I'm the flow in this shadeless cold meadow

the death of an old fox will leave the territory
    free
for a hungry cub
this fox can see into the future.

Reproduction

It is difficult to identify the sex of a mole, as the external male and female sex organs are almost identical. The female has a clitoris which is as large as the male's penis, about 3mm long; it's pink, and if you squeeze the mole's belly it pops out and is easy to see, but she doesn't have a vaginal opening.

In the past people used to believe that all moles were males until the breeding season, when half of them would become female. I have read that the females are true hermaphrodites: they have ovaries but they also have testes that produce testosterone, which for most of the year makes them aggressive toward intruders and protective of their territory. However, in the breeding season less testosterone is produced, and the female will allow males to approach and mate. Her falling testosterone levels cause her to develop a vagina. After giving birth her testosterone increases, her vagina closes up, and she becomes aggressive again.

In the breeding season around February the female will build a nest in her tunnel system about the size of a football, which she lines with leaves and twigs. Moles have a terrific sense of smell, and over some distance the males will sniff her out in her den, dig a tunnel straight toward her, or even travel overground, I am told. They mate, and then the males run off to look for other mates. When the breeding season is over the males all return to their solitary lives in their own original tunnel systems. Twenty-nine days later, around April or May, the female will give birth to three or four young kits. They are naked, and will stay in the nest drinking their mother's milk until they start to eat live food. The mother begins to produce testosterone again soon after their birth. Her maternal instincts fade, and in late spring, when the kits are five or six weeks old, her parenting is done, and she chases the young out of her tunnel system. They wander blindly on the grass for a while looking for food. Most of the young will be eaten by birds at this time. The homeless of all species are predated.

Nature produces millions of everything and it fills in all the gaps. Nature doesn't care about a single individual; it is easy to just make more, billions more. Each human, mole and dragonfly, each dandelion and blade of grass, wears out and is replaced. Once life has got going it is cheap and easy for nature to sustain, as all living things are programmed to reproduce. If a population outstrips its food supply because of a high birth rate or a drought, for instance, many die until some kind of balance is achieved.

Eventually the surviving moles will start a tunnel of their own, perhaps by digging for shelter from the birds, or they will move into tunnels left vacant by moles that were trapped last year or died some other way. They start their independent lives, and I am called to come and catch them as they start to work repairing tunnels and building new ones. A mole's life is full of struggle. They stay where they are, eating and sleeping, and then they die, and another mole moves in and takes their place, and runs around the maze eating and sleeping. Once you have learned this, they are easy to catch.

The average life span of a mole is around four years: they will see four mating seasons, and when they have produced offspring they, like all living creatures, are no longer needed. The average life span of a human in the UK is 81.6 years. The average age that humans stop having sex is around 70. The average age at which human children leave home changes all the time, depending on the job market. At the moment in the UK it is between 20 and 34.

The muddy river to my right is flowing high and fast now. It has rained a lot this winter, but the field here is dry and frosty today. The Brecon Beacons, about fifty miles to the north, are draining their sodden dark earth. There is more rain coming, I can smell it. The heavy river pushes grey and muddy over deeply hidden rocks that show above the water in the summer when it's low and green with slowly waving weed, like a drowned woman's hair.

I am dressed in thick cotton moleskin, velvety and muddied, in a field bounded by stones, with crows hanging over bits of sheep fleece hanging on the wire fence. The soft wind turns and brushes my skin.

At fifteen, when I left school in the coal-blackened North, I escaped the life of a mole: I was 'too tall' at six feet two. The mine boss said I would crack my skull and break my back. My father, who ran the village pub, tried to get me down there to scrape coal from the walls like the strong and stocky short-armed men around me. The hidden lone mole draws my interest but we are not the same, the mole and me. I didn't fit in the hole. I was apprenticed to work with steel instead, welding, cutting, drilling, rolling and bending massive steel plates. I didn't stay there very long. Less than a year. I was pushed from the nest. I walked; there was no scent of home.

*

I am drawn back to that wandering outdoor life and when I retire from working the earth, which is not too far away now, I think about loading up my backpack and walking across it again for a while. But I can't bear to spend too long away from Peggy. As I get older and my life grows slow and comfortable I often think about the bittersweet joy and simple freedom of living outdoors, wrapped in a blanket on a pile of dry twigs or leaves and looking up through the leaves of a small hedgerow oak and into the sky as the night falls, watching the silhouette of the blackbird singing from the topmost branch of the tree.

That was a life without worry. I would live or die and neither would matter. Even lying under a pier once, starving and feeling that I was dying, I felt sad, but I also reasoned that it was perfectly acceptable to feel sad in that situation. Goodbyes are sad. There is no avoiding sadness in life, although it seems that happiness is easier to avoid. I have in my time deliberately tried to die, but I am still here, and life has always won on its own terms, so I stopped trying to make the choice for myself. It seemed that it was not my decision to make, and I began allowing life to happen. It feels much better that way. I learned it from the birds, who just flew and nested and ate and made new birds, and the hedgehogs, who just shuffled and ate and made new hedgehogs, and they all died and went back to mud in their own good time.

Having worked all my life, created a family, discovered a home, I feel as secure as a working-class man ever feels, and I feel a sense of equality again with the crow and the toad and the hawthorn, with the rain and wind. I am them and they are me. I lost my self-importance early on and do not want to differentiate myself from the world around me. I am just another animal, another tree, another wild flower in the meadow among billions of others, each unique in their own way, each just like the others in other ways, each one just another expression of nature trying to survive. There is something deeply magnificent in being just ordinary.

I know how to survive in the kind of nature that constantly circles around me, and I am in love with it. I trust it to behave in the way it always behaves, and I expect it to be dangerous. Nature does not care about our safety. To be comfortable and safe I have learned to be aware, and to do this I have to quieten my internal dialogue, to trust my body to tell me if something is wrong. To do that I have to listen, and be alone.

Twilight and the sky turns brass
Instead of going home to hearth I want to stay
out under branches to watch the night
arrive on a cold stone wall
long after I can see

the darkness when it comes is final
like death, yet not so quiet
small things move about
the sleeping larger things and rustle
only the smallest things bite

I like to sleep in these woods
like my ancestors
sleeping in the land of animals
vagrant
dreaming with the birds

held by a life in its strong old branches
curled at the base of a mossy oak tree
watching the last light fade
twigs scratch against the flat
cold December sky and I
feel safe.

Oxygen

Moles live in a dark, damp atmosphere that has little oxygen. Tunnelling is hard work, and working muscles demand lots of oxygen. The haemoglobin in the blood of a mole can hold far more oxygen than the blood of other animals, and, uniquely, a mole can re-breathe its own breath, extracting as much life from it as possible. The downside is that mole blood is poor at clotting and moles easily bleed to death. I hear that researchers have been looking at how a genetically modified version of mole blood could be used in humans and I wonder what the scientists may have in mind.

When I kneel on the ground and open a mole tunnel, the system is suddenly flushed with fresh air. The mole, wherever he is, is quickly aware of this, and will assume that a weasel or a stoat has got into the tunnel and is coming to eat him, so he'll try to establish which direction the fresh air is coming from and immediately backfill the tunnel. It is an automatic response; there is no choice to be made. Like all creatures, except humans and dogs, they run away from danger, so if I want to catch him I need to move quickly and confuse him with air entering in other places, so that he doesn't know in what direction the breach was made.

I work in a broad-brimmed waxed-cotton hat that I have worn for years. It used to be green, now it is brown with dried earth and it smells of the damp ground. Old photographs of molecatchers always show them wearing a battered, broad-brimmed hat. This hat is part of the toolkit. If it's raining it helps to keep me dry while I look at the territory during my survey, but its primary function is to quickly cover the holes I make to prevent light and more oxygen getting in.

I try to avoid working in the rain. Mud sticks to the tools, and it's hard to work the earth when it's raining. It can also, if I am in the wrong frame of mind, turn the mind dark if I find myself kneeling in a thunderstorm in a muddy field with clods of mud sticking to me while I pull soggy dead moles out of their holes with cold wet hands. Although at times that happens because once the traps are in the ground I want to visit them every day, and if the weather changes I just have to work in it.

Walking past the dripping holly trees at the end of the field, the leaves shine with a dark labial wetness, as slick and black as engine oil in the shade as the frost melts. They splash my face as I brush past. The holly berries bright and clean light up against the darkness, and inside the tree's shade a robin perches and sings so loudly, shouting out his ownership of his territory. In the branches an old starling's nest, a Carlsberg can, a crisp packet (cheese and onion). Around the base of the tree a ring of very old molehills, collapsed and with dandelions and creeping buttercup growing in them. It will take years for the grass to repopulate these old hills. Moles throw soil onto the surface, which deprives the grass it lands on of light, and so it dies. This soil will contain seeds and, whatever the weather, within a few weeks of a molehill appearing, it will be sprouting weeds of some kind. Some seeds can live for many years underground until conditions are right for germination. Scientists have not yet found the limit – I read recently of seeds over 1,000 years old germinating. Grass rarely gets the chance to set seed before it is mown or grazed, so it can spread only by sending up new shoots from existing roots; the space in the molehills will be taken by weeds long before that can happen.

There are surface tunnels here, coiling on the earth. I walk past them; I have never had any success catching moles in surface tunnels. But further in the field the network runs deeper.

The robin in the holly tree is a tiny bird, yet must be one of the bravest creatures. He is no more than half a metre away from me, and stops singing and cocks his head at me to focus with his left eye, then stares at me full-on with both. For a while we just look at each other. Then he starts shouting again and I move on, still walking the edges of the field. Before I have moved far, he has overtaken me and is perched in a willow, and is singing in front of me again. Robins have

learned that people disturb the soil, so they follow us looking for food. I am always happy to see them, and sometimes feel that perhaps an individual recognises me from my last visit.

A cormorant perhaps, but brown-headed – I thought they were all black – shows me his tail when he sees me on the bank, and downstream he goes. There are no people to watch, to see, or to know that I am here in the early light with the singing birds. There is winter sun and websilk woven through the silhouetted branches, and it sparkles like rippling water.

I have identified a number of mole territories: most of them are around the edges of the field, and there will be some main tunnels under the trees. The moles are very active here. As I walk I catch over my right shoulder a man standing watching, but when I turn to greet him there is nobody there. This happens to me often as I get older. Perhaps it is me coming back to watch.

My leaf-capped boots leave footprints in the frosty grass, and I'm thankful to be old; I can rest and take my time and it is okay. It is good to be old, and good to be slow, and have nothing left to fear or gain or lose – I can just dance if I want, and sleep if I want. I turn at the bottom of the field and head back up. The long, labyrinthine walk again. I imagine myself to be a minotaur. I blow steam from my nose.

Through the prison of bare ash trees the blue frosted hills glow in the distance. My home is here. It is still, the frost bites my skin and I love her for that nip. The auburn leaves crackle. There is no breeze now, the sky naked, undressed, and so too is the earth I am standing on. Waiting. A high white streak. It looks slow from down here, but is travelling fast to some warmer place, perhaps? There are people all the way up there, excited people travelling.

I look down again and carry on walking back to the top of the field where I left my traps and other tools.

We are getting older, Peggy and me, and we have made a home and a life together and I want to be there. We are free. We can eat whenever we want. We can go wherever we can afford to go without asking anybody. We can sleep face to face and not touching, but breathing each other's breath over and over until there is no oxygen left between us, and one of us has at last to turn away or die. We have grown to love each other more over the years. Peggy said we are doing it back to front – that we should have loved each other passionately at the beginning and it should have faded away by now into grumpy middle age. That is nature's way of preparing us to be separated, she said. Then she got sad, and she said that sadness is the price we pay for love, as her eyes teared up and her pretty face cracked at thoughts of age and death and one of us losing the other.

Right here at the edge of change I know that my gardening days are coming to an end because my own life is slowing, cooling. I will miss seeing the coupling dragonflies as long as my forearm that have buzzed me as I have worked. The hawkmoth caterpillar on my palm, as big as my index finger, that raised itself up in defiance; the hawks that circle as they hunt the field mice who run ahead for their little burrows exposed by the falling stalks as I cut them. The grass snakes that sleep on the compost heap under its tarpaulin cover; the toad that lives at the bottom of the wall; the slow worms hunting in the leaf litter; the snails that sleep in families in curled leaves, or clustered together like nuts in gaps in walls.

Peggy wants me to stop doing this work; she worries about me out here where there is no mobile-phone reception. She worries that 'something will happen' to me and nobody will be able to find me. I don't tell anybody where I am going each day; my diary is on my phone and is with me. In the shadow of the hills I have no signal. I am a ghost, and instead of just enjoying my work I am thinking about the possibility of dropping to the ground, and who would find me? I am forced to contemplate death, I am growing older, I have a heart problem, I get exhausted easily. These thoughts affect my mood and I remind myself that nothing is perfect, nothing is complete, and nothing is ever finished. I write a little poem about it on my phone:

My head an old brown jug
stuffed with dry leaves
rustling and scraping thoughts
worthless noise

My feet old boots full of mud
going nowhere
#molecatcher

I can't think of a better place to spend my last hours. I watch a seed spin and fall from a tree onto the frost: it has no meaning – then the robin sings at my feet again as I walk, and the sun hits my back, and slowly I lose my train of thought, and become happy again.

I remember to accept the not-knowing because it is unknowable, and to let my mind clear, the thoughts pass, and allow myself to be filled with the quiet nature that is alive with possibility and fertility. I think of it as 'going primordial', back into the soup that I came from. There is something sacred in putting one foot in front of the other, over and over again, for a lifetime. To eat, walk and sleep. To walk this field and look for moles, to pay the bills, to spend our days and nights together.

I remember waking on a bed of pine needles at the edge of a wood, and looking into the morning as the sun rose over a field. There was a perfect moment as the floor and lower branches, the trunks and stems and bits of undergrowth, turned gold and bright. A burning, horizontal light cast long shadows of trunks down the rows between the managed trees before, too quickly, the sun climbed above the branches and sent the edge of the wood back into shade again. Perfection is always brief. I went looking for the other edge of the wood that day, so that I could spend the night and see it happen again as the sun went down on the other side, but I think there must have been cloud that night, because I can only remember the looking, but not the finding. As I think about that golden light, a flood of other waking memories comes. Pearls on a string.

One freezing cold morning I woke on a riverside, and, opening my eyes in thick fog, I could not see anything at all but a little glow through the white mist – I stood up with my blanket around me; it was covered with millions of water droplets clinging to its hairy surface. I rose through the mist that came up to my chest and looked down on its swirling surface. It was so dense that I could not see my feet. The river had flood defences built up on the outside of the riverside paths, and as the sun came up I could see the mist stretching across the valley from side to side as far along as I could see. The tops of the trees and shrubs were sticking up out of the fog into the clear sky, and the rising sun was casting the shadows of the trees on top of the mist. It was perhaps one of the most beautiful things I have ever seen. Even now, over 45 years later, I see it as clear as if it had happened this morning.

I gathered my things and walked through it, like a boat leaving a wake rippling in the fog behind me, and as the day warmed up I walked myself dry.

*

When I was young I wanted to know everything
now I am old I want to know nothing
what I have is of no use
at the end the only truth is the breath
overcome with lust to grab this moment
with all of my senses before it passes

why fight to shine a light
when the vastness all around is dark?
it makes no sense
I'll simply tend my lamp
I may see something of myself
perhaps
reflected

on the ridge two fields away a tractor.
the driver waves a hand and I wave back
my heart leaps, a feeling of joy
I suddenly want to run to say hello
I've not seen another man for days
begun to lose my words

I've heard no human voice
not even my own

I learned so many years ago to growl
to speak in grunts and chirps
to keep all kinds of predators away

are antlers pressing through my bald cold skull?
I'm moving breath and heartbeat, little more.
I cough to make a noise, to feel that I am real

A pheasant explodes loudly from the grass
a farm dog begins barking in the distance
the only message carried by these sounds is

'I am here.'

Gas and the Dead Past

The threat of rain has passed for now but it will be back by the end of the day. The air is still. There's no music of waves, no wind or rain to sing to me. Even the buzzing in my ears has faded. But there is scent, something dead, somewhere near.

A single rook spreads his fingers in slow flight across my horizon-spanning sky. It is December and the mole-catching season is in full flow. The melancholy passes and only in noticing its passing do I become aware that it was there in the first place, and I wonder why, and when it came. Then the wondering passes, as does the day, heading into afternoon. The time is hard to gauge. The sun rises and stays low and flat above the cloud, and toward the late afternoon falls again quickly, I notice the temperature dipping before the sky brightens as the sun drops below the cloud. The fallen leaves are sweet and rich-smelling as they turn back into earth. Our scents mingle, our essences mix. I sniff the air for signs of rain. It is there, but distant.

A mole's sense of smell is its most powerful faculty. Moles have a primitive brain: smooth, without corrugations or wrinkles, like a snake's, like a liver or a kidney. Smell is the most primitive sense, the most powerful and evocative. If we lose our sense of smell we lose much of our sense of taste too. My nose is always blocked, I can taste little. I can still smell rain and powerful rotting things, but subtler things are lost to me. Growing older is a process of shutting down. In decay I see the beginning of growth, because that is how I choose to see the world, because it makes the world elegant and poetic; because I have no religion; because I am a gardener and I see it every day.

I remember Peggy telling me that I smell beautiful, of smoky old whisky and fresh sweat and oil. I work in nature and I smell of it. At different times of the year I smell of different things: of grass, lavender, rotting wood, fresh-cut pine, rain, rotting leaves, old wide river, rain on hot stone, wet wool, mud. Dogs and cats can't get enough of me. I am invisible to wildlife because I smell like them. Birds and insects land on me. I take ladybirds home nesting in my collar. I like to be invisible.

When I was a small child I saw a picture in a school Bible (we were never religious) of St Francis with birds perched on him and animals at his feet. I wanted to be like that, and I practised standing perfectly still and breathing softly. I felt that I could stand like that for hours, like a tree. When I was living with the birds I would sit or move quietly for hours, days even, hoping that the animals would feel safe with me. Now, forty-odd years later, robins land on my warm boot and watch me when I sit on the grass to eat my lunch.

Robins are decorative and people love them, but people do not feel the same way about moles. Humans have tried every way imaginable to get rid of them. But moles are eternal and ceaseless. Moles in most places are caught with traps, but in private places, away from buildings and where children and animals do not go – places that can be closed off, and that employ permanent ground staff, like golf courses, for instance – they are often poisoned, by a member of staff who is trained and licensed to put piles of aluminium phosphide pellets in the tunnels. As the pellets draw moisture from the soil they give off poisonous phosphine gas, which supposedly flows through the tunnels. There is little airflow in a tunnel, so it probably pools in the low points. Phosphine gas can cause a slow, painful death, taking hours or days, especially if the mole is at a distant part of the run and the dose he receives is small. In humans, phosphine gas produces difficulty in breathing, burns the eyes, nose and throat, causes nausea and vomiting. Skin contact causes burns, and with high enough concentrations fluid builds up in the lungs within a few hours and ends in a choking, drowning death around 24 hours later. Things poisoned in an uncontrolled environment such as a field rarely 'just go to sleep peacefully', as people may like to believe: the dose the animal actually receives is unknowable, and suffering is inevitable.

The hidden moles are gassed unknown to the golfers above, and so the problem molehills just disappear. The golfers see no traps, no dead moles or molecatchers, and the whole messy business of killing carries on discreetly.

There have been well-recorded instances of families of children accidentally breathing in this gas and being killed because rat runs near their home were being poisoned with phosphine gas which leaked out of cracks in the earth. There is no known antidote.

Under a bush I find the dead thing that I have been smelling. A fox. It still has plenty of fur, so it hasn't been dead for very long. He looks like an old boy, and he has reached the end of his days here under a laurel. He has chosen a good place.

The laurel is thick and well grown, and as a gardener I usually cut and shape laurel hedges at the end of the summer. Traditionally in August. This gives them enough time to put out new leaves before the winter comes and slows their growth. If I cut laurel at the right time I only have to do it once a year: if I were to cut it in the spring I would have to do it again before the year was out. The leaves are big and shiny, and if I trimmed them with the petrol hedge cutter they would get shattered, torn and ugly, so to keep it neat and natural-looking it has to be pruned by hand. The best way is branch by branch with hand secateurs, but few customers want to pay for this, as it is time-consuming and therefore expensive. I am lucky and have such customers. I have one laurel hedge that takes three days to cut; when it's finished it looks lovely. When I am hand-pruning I always try to make it look as if I haven't been there: I make the cuts close to a leaf or branch joint, so there are no bare stems poking out and it looks natural. After this repetitive and heavy work with secateurs my right hand will no longer work properly for a while. My fingers lock into a claw, because the tendons that move my fingers are too swollen to run cleanly through their sheaths. By the next spring my hand is usually back to normal.

Cut laurel releases the scent of almonds because the leaves and branches contain cyanide, and unwitting gardeners have been overcome by this in the past. When I smell it powerfully it is time to step away and let the air disperse the gas. On a still day the cyanide lingers in the branches of the hedge.

The low sun breaks through bare branches and they glow. Small twigs crack and fall around me. There is a buzzard circling above, and small birds are flitting around, scattered. The shadows are pink again. Cherry trees stand still against the grim December sky. A broken cloud of small birds can't make up its mind which tree. Another bird, silhouetted, is singing at the pinnacle of the pine tree's spire. He is loud and alone against the grey of cloud and the passing sound of small rain.

The texture of this place is flattened and monochrome for winter. An iron Welsh sky, and over the hills coal-black cloud loaded, heavy and waiting. As temporary and fragile as a bubble, and wrapped in wool, I'm walking through bare branches turned to sunlight. Working my way along the hedgerows, in the places where the fox goes. Over the way a field of Highland cattle remind me of my boyhood in a tartan kilt that my Scottish grandmother used to like to dress me in. I cried when my father said I couldn't wear it any more – I was about seven, or five? And I wonder about this memory: it's not a clear one, from so long ago, and I wonder if it is actually mine, or one I picked up from a film or a story? Wasn't there a photograph of me, aged about five, dressed in my bright kilt and long grey socks and polished chestnut brown brogues, holding my Nana's hand? Walking in a parade? There is nobody left from the unreliable past who can tell me. I have no family photographs. Nevertheless, I have taken the memory as mine and use it as my own.

Huddled up one night against a drystone wall near Pendle Hill, where there is an Iron Age burial mound and witches were caught and sent for hanging. The 'Pen' of Pendle is a Cymric word for 'hill', a relic in Lancashire of the language of the Old North that is still vividly alive in much of Wales. I was screwed tight in a tarpaulin with just a gap for my eyes and mouth, watching and listening to the rain slam down on the hill and run down in torrents from the black clouds that seemed as if they would never pass through a night that might never end. It is simple, and perhaps obvious, that it was almost unbearably beautiful and equally unbearably lonely. That night left me with the understanding that these two feelings do not conflict with each other. Like the overwhelming and unbearable, yet ultimately borne feeling of grief at losing a loved one.

There is a sense of being connected with history when leaning against or working with these old stone stock walls, some of them established over 4,000 years ago by Neolithic people, the first people on these islands to protect grain crops from animals or to enclose beasts for the night.

Sometimes in such places it is easy to become aware of the lives of the people who bent over these walls and built and repaired them for many generations. The walls are benign, they have no function other than to keep animals in or out. I never feared the ancient dead as I walked alone and slept under the sky in these old places, but sometimes it felt as if they were not long gone – just over the hill, perhaps. Many years later I went into the mountains with a team of drystone wallers, and for a week learned how to make and repair these walls.

Occasionally, when I thought I was alone, there would be a disturbance in the atmosphere, a sensation that somebody was nearby, and my senses would go into overdrive, spreading about from me at their centre like fingers into the darkness, searching, and either the feeling would pass and I would go back to resting, or it wouldn't, and I would stay alert and wide awake until it was light enough to leave.

There were some places that gave me a bad feeling in the spine or the back of the head. Walking under a small brick road bridge that passed over a canal, a place that might have been a choice place to sleep for the night if it was raining: that sent the hairs standing up on my neck. I moved through that place quickly. There were other places that felt very good, warm and kind, which I felt very sad to leave. A small wood that I reached by climbing a stile and crossing a field, I have no idea where. There were boulders pressing through the earth; they were warm. It was so pleasant I could have just stayed there and returned to earth with the litter; perhaps the desire to stay in a place that had no food or water made it a dangerous place too, but eventually the need to move overcame the desire to stay.

I have no theories about why those good and bad feelings happened. I have become a pragmatist about such things, and no longer try to understand them. Life is so full of mystery, answers are so few, I do not trust them. I prefer unanswered questions. At the end of the answers there is usually a person who enjoys the power of appearing to know. I have come to like things that are left unfinished. It's the question that shines the light, that seeks. The answer's often just a dim reflection of the vastness of the question. There are no answers that satisfy.

This is a small life, and everything comes to nothing in the end. I like that. I like the idea of smallness, and the wonder of basic human things.

In these hard and empty hills where all there is
     to do
is to fight and love
I've learned to love to fight

I found my wholeness in learning not to seek
it's here in the wind that blows
me like a crow to my chosen place

my friend rook, the cleverest of all the creatures
teaches how to fight without fighting
he lets go in the strong wind

he plays and blown about
looking ragged and broken
he lands to rest then up he goes again.

I have heard that wind can drive you mad
not me, I've taken off my jacket
so that I can feel it plucking at my shirt and skin.

maybe it has already taken my mind
maybe that is why I love it.

Poison and Winter

About sixty years ago molecatchers were threatened by the arrival of the mole-killers, who would offer to clear the moles from a farmer's land for a fraction of the price a traditional molecatcher would charge. They carried a jam jar of worms around, and killed the moles by placing these worms soaked in strychnine in the mole tunnels. The mole-killers were despised by the traditional molecatchers: they took business away and had no skills, no heritage, no craft. They were seen as money-minded grubby poisoners. They gave no evidence of having killed the moles they were after, and there was a long-term risk of the whole population of moles being destroyed. The craft of hunting was for a while replaced by the chemical science of mass killing.

The poison did not kill the worms, but anything that ate them took up the poison in smaller or larger amounts. Strychnine is a horrible poison that was responsible for the secondary slow poisoning of domestic animals and birds of prey who ate the worms or a dead mole. A domestic cat catching a dying bird that had eaten a poisoned worm would succumb to a very slow and painful death.

In 2006, despite the British government's strong protests and lobbying from the mole-killers, it was banned by the European Union for any use whatsoever because of its danger to the environment. Mole-killers lost their income. Strychnine is not used any more, traditional molecatchers once again find work in farms and gardens, and the balance of power is restored.

I use a whetstone to hone the blades and knives I use in my work. It was engineered to be hard and perfectly flat when I bought it years ago, but now has a smooth complex curve that tells the story of how I use it. A tool responds to the way it is used. Slowly over time it just naturally changes its shape to fit in with the way I do things. I just like to look at it sometimes. To hold it in my hand.

While the knife wears away the stone, the stone also wears away the knife and over time their curves become matched. People do that too: when Peggy and I met we were scratchy and brittle and fought a lot, but over the years we have worn off each other's spines, smoothed out the roughness, and our curves now match.

Before her, I waved to the blind and sang to the deaf. Then Peggy came and she sang and waved back. We are both vagrants, and I realise that all the time that I was growing up with her and being selfish, solitary and afraid, she was waiting for me in the dark without me knowing. She was a better hunter than I. While she told me fairy stories about lost children who became found, she was describing how she found me and watched me grow. This tattooed, battered, hair-matted hand with its plain iron bracelet was tied with a coloured ribbon to hers for ever. Cariad.

In my pocket a pencil that was once five inches long, now just a stump. Blunted, writing my story. Nothing is ever finished. I think it will soon be time for me to pick up the worn blade honed on the worn stone, sharpen the old stump to a point, and start to scratch a new chapter, a new life.

As I walked through the seasons and the weather I carried few things, and the things I did carry wore out as I was starting to wear out. I went hungry, sometimes very hungry, and I feared for my life, but those times were few, and I became very good at keeping myself safe. I slipped away from the predators and the paedophiles who hung around the towns and sniffed around me like charming rats. The man who offered me a hot meal and a bed as I wandered into Blackpool, who 'looked after lots of boys like me', and the well-dressed woman who pulled up next to me in the early hours along a deserted street outside Manchester and tried to get me into her car: 'Do you want to go to a party?' I smelled danger, I moved on. Towns are fun and exciting, but they are dangerous. People want things, they crave experiences.

Eventually my socks wore out and my boots got holes, and I learned the value of wool. Wool will keep you warm even if it is wet. Wet cotton, nylon or feathers will kill you. My expensive down sleeping-bag got soaked in a downpour and would not keep me warm. Wet, it was too heavy to carry. I hung it on branches hoping it would dry, and I slept wrapped in my coat for a few days. It was a useless luxury item, and I dumped it in a bin and bought an old wool blanket from a charity shop that became very precious to me. It was blue and rough and warm, and even when wet it was still warm, and when it got wet it dried again. That blue blanket became my most important possession. I do not remember what happened to it. I wish sometimes that I still had it, just to hold it, like a baby.

I missed a hot drink from time to time. Occasionally if I had the money I would wander into a village, find a breakfast café and buy a coffee, an egg on toast. Sometimes when I had no money left I ate bread and milk stolen from doorsteps in the early hours like a bird, biscuits from a grocer's, or a tin of beans opened with my Swiss army knife. I never did manage to get hold of a spoon or a fork to eat them with.

Over time my pack got lighter as I discarded things I didn't use – a camp stove and the pots and pans, a tent – and I gathered other things I needed: a water bottle, a blanket, a tarpaulin. Having to carry my whole world in a rucksack taught me quickly the difference between wants and needs. I missed books. I missed having socks. I threw away my worn-out boots and walked in tennis shoes. When I walked I shed all of my encumbrances, I carried only what was necessary. I have given in a little now as I have grown older and softer; I buy too many clothes and books.

All the small things put a blanket around the
   earth
all the small things in their infinite variety blanket
   round this rocky wet earth
all the small things are the things that blanket, the
   things that warm.
the things that feed
the things that eat
all the small things, microscopic dots of life of
   cells that blanket trickle flow and feed this
   rocky layered stone of earth
all the small things die
then live, then die again
and feed and build the blanket layers on this
   rocky stone of earth
and in their living and their dying and their living
   and their dying
and their eating and their feeding and their dying
   and their breeding and their growing, they
   build this rocky stone of earth

Deterrents

I live close enough to the river to be able to walk in an hour or so from our house and along its banks past the castle and into the middle of Cardiff. My two children are grown up and have homes of their own; it is just Peggy and me now, and when I am out working I miss her and want to go home.

My children are scattered, taken on the breeze and growing well in fertile soil. Peggy and I created them, and they are part of the growing population that is causing the expansion of towns and pollution and the loss of countryside that makes us fearful for the future. It would be easy to mourn or hope that science will fix it. We are a fearful species.

There are a lot of open spaces in the world. The Highlands of Scotland are sparsely populated apart from the immense herds of deer which sweep across the landscape, devouring everything in sight, because we have killed the wolves that used to manage their numbers. Further south in the towns and cities there is not much wild space left for us to enjoy.

I learned as a boy that nature has no interest in our enjoyment or our survival. Unless we are protected and entertained like children we have to actively engage with our own survival and find our own enjoyment. People talk of the fight for survival, but it is not a fight, it is a conversation. There's a negotiation that goes on. The word 'fighting' implies that there is some kind of aggression involved, but aggressive behaviour will eventually put you in the food chain of something bigger, stronger, and faster. The 'fight' for survival is a conversation with one's self: learning to accept and live with hunger and cold, exhaustion, difficulties and fear, and still keep going because the alternative is to stop and die, or become dependent like a child.

Survival is about being aware of danger, assessing how dangerous it is and stepping aside from it. If you get that decision wrong, and keep going when you should stop, you may be victorious or you may not; either way it will cost you. Submission rarely works when confronted by aggressive creatures or humans, but when it comes to bad weather the only thing to be done is to avoid or submit.

The fox scratches the ticks off his back, the cat cleans mud off his feet, moles clean their tunnels. People try to keep their property tidy. They put hoses on their exhaust pipes and try to gas the moles, pour diesel fuel down the burrows, set light to molehills with petrol, fire shotguns, pour bleach, stick mothballs, garlic and other 'mole-repelling plants' and unpleasant substances into the holes. I meet people who have tried all these things and more. But if a mole comes across something it doesn't like, he either digs it out and pushes it to the surface, or he blocks the tunnel and digs around the problem. Undefeated, he makes more molehills. He is a master of survival strategy, the first rule of which is 'Take a detour around the dangerous thing'.

Windmills and electronic scarers some-times seem to work for a while. But the moles learn that these things are benign, and they come back. Once I was looking at a fabulous new mole scarer that whistled and vibrated, when I saw it start to move, and slowly get pushed out of the tunnel, fall over and lie on the ground screaming and shaking, while the mole repaired the hole it came from. Moles are quite happy living in public parks by football fields and motorway verges. Noise and vibration-makers, no matter how elaborate, are devices for taking money from frustrated humans rather than scaring moles.

What moles really dislike is compacted soil. Fields where there are cattle usually only have molehills around the fence lines where the cattle don't tread. Sports fields regularly rolled with a heavy roller and aerated are rarely troubled with moles. I had a regular customer who was in the building trade who I told about this, so he drove around on his lawn with a road roller, and the moles left and never came back; they moved next door. I lost one customer, gained another, angrier one.

I spot two red horses galloping unsaddled, unfettered across the ridge, throwing long fast shadows across the frosted grass, and I stand and watch them and want to be them, although my body is now too old and worn to run. I remember running cross-country when I was at school: we ran in black gym shoes, plimsolls, on fells through mud and streams. I was not fast, but could go on for longer than anybody else. I didn't want to stop.

There is much birdsong in the trees and hedgerows; I can hear it this afternoon. A *peep peep peep peep* and a *chitterwijee, chitterwijee* and many others. I can hear the calls of four, maybe five different birds looking for mates or defending their territories. I don't know their names or which song belongs to which bird, apart from those brave enough to sit and sing by me, the robin and the blackbirds, and of course I know the crows, magpies, gulls and pigeons. But the smaller flocking birds are just flitting, singing clouds. Once I was a curiosity or a threat to them. Now I am so familiar I have become invisible. I am nobody, and so I have reached the pinnacle of my existence.

*

If you want to catch a live mole you can buy a humane trap. This is usually a metal, or more often plastic, tube that is put into the tunnel. It has a one-way flap at either end: the mole goes into it and cannot get out again. If you catch a living mole using a humane trap, you have to decide where to release him. He will have been in that trap for a period of time. It will take more time to transport him, in distress, to a release site. If he cannot find food quickly he will become weak and die.

On the ground he moves relatively slowly, slower if he is hungry. He is fat, he squirms and is conspicuous, so he has to get below ground quickly before he is eaten. Moles can't live in ground that is too hard, too soft, too wet or too dry, so he will need to find the kind of earth that moles like. If you catch a live mole and don't put him back where you caught him, you are condemning him to a slow death.

People have asked me about keeping a mole as a pet. If you want to keep him as a pet, you will need to supply him with worms at a phenomenal rate, and you will never see him. If you wanted him to have a good life, instead of a short miserable one, you would need a tank full of good soil, about two feet deep and as big as the floor plan of a house.

The sunlight breaks through the bare branches, and they shine gold for a while. Over on the windless hill white with frost four miles away I can see white, still windmills waiting. Everything is waiting. Except the mole, who, warm and deep, keeps eating and digging.

I am back at the top of the field now, having walked my route. There are plenty of moles to catch, and over the field boundaries there are more to repopulate the field in the spring. I could come and trap here every year for a lifetime. I go to the edge of the first territory, kneel on the ground and prepare my tools: put my knee pads on, knock the soil out of a handful of traps, take out my trowel, spade and mole probe.

I walk beside a trickling steam with muddy banks
to a pool of rotting leaves,
of sparkling life I wouldn't want
to put my hand in
I look into that slimy little pond
where spiny pincered bugs breed
and bubbles burst
from under stinking leaves
where corpses rot
and I find at last
my own reflection

and in the pool
a hunter's wind-browned rain-blasted bearded face
skin stretched tight over sharpening bones
stares back at me
and even a child knows
that the way to truly disappear from the world
is to shut your eyes tight
and not let anything in

then over my shoulder
the sun strikes off the water
bleaches my reflection
and warms my face
I feel kissed on the forehead
like a child alone
There are feathers everywhere.

Mole Traps and Breaking Things

Before I start probing for trap sites I kneel in the mud on the ground outside of the active area and set a handful of traps. There is a lot of kneeling: this field is my church. The ground is wet; you rarely find moles in dry ground. I wear moleskin trousers that are crusty with the dried earth from yesterday's work (moleskin fabric is made of heavy hardwearing cotton; it is like thick corduroy without the stripes). I press down the spring-powered catching loop with the barrel pressed into my belly, hold the pressure of the killing spring and flip over the loose trip hook to stop the loop closing again, catch it behind the mumble pin – and the trap is set. It takes two hands: the spring is strong and could, perhaps, take off a finger.

I like these words: 'trip hook', 'mumble pin', 'catching loop'. They give me a sense of tradition, a feeling of connectedness with the ancient history of this craft, a sense of some kind of 'belonging' in a world that works hard to take that sense away.

Mole traps have been around since the Romans used them to protect their crops and pleasure gardens. Early Roman mole traps were a simple clay pot with a hole halfway up the side. The hole meant that the pot would remain half-filled with water. The pot was sunk into the tunnel, the mole would fall in and, unable to climb out, would swim around and around until, exhausted, he drowned.

Later, itinerant molecatchers would make their own traps that caught the moles around the waist in a loop of twine powered by a springy wooden stick. The mole would have to be killed later by hand. Then more sophisticated traps came along, made from pottery tubes, again with string or wire catching loops. Other, more recent traps drove sharp iron spikes down into the mole as it passed underneath.

Modern mole traps come in many designs. I and most other molecatchers use two different kinds of traps: scissor traps and half-barrel traps, based closely on some of the early wooden and pottery traps. Both are efficient killers. Good modern traps are expensive: they are designed and tuned to deliver the most powerful blow possible to the right part of the mole as quickly as possible.

I use the half-barrel trap more than any other. It looks like half a metal tube about six inches long and three wide. The half-tube forms the roof of the mole tunnel when it's put in the ground. There are steel wire loops at either end which are pressed into the soil on the floor of the tunnel, and can catch a mole as it enters from either end. The two loops have powerful coil springs which make them snap up explosively against the roof of the trap, stopping the mole's heart when it hits the trigger. They are efficient and deadly.

Scissor traps, again powered by coil springs, sit across the tunnel and, when the mole hits the trigger, a pair of steel claws snaps shut from either side of the tunnel across the mole's chest, killing it. I use scissor traps from time to time in places where access is difficult – under walls or paths, for instance, as they are much smaller. I also use them when I have run out of tunnel traps because they are all in the ground. At times I have had over a hundred traps in the ground at once. Traps do not need any kind of bait: they are triggered by the mole just wandering through it on his way to find something to eat.

To catch your mole, buy three half-barrel traps. You will need at least three. Buy the best and most expensive ones that you can find. Killing a living thing should not be cheap or slow.

Buddhists say that life is full of sadness and the only way to live with it is through compassion. They say that we should feel both sadness and joy in everything we do. There is a joy in being in this field, being like the hawk or the hedgehog. There is a sadness in it, too, in the journey from the place where we start to the place where we end. Mine is not a journey that goes anywhere or delivers anything of any importance, it just goes. Like a poppy it emerges, flowers and fades, then dries and turns to dust. Compassion is born at the interaction between joy and sadness. Compassion for your own life, forgiveness for your own mistakes, is the foundation.

There is always sadness. I once heard a friend, depressed, under the influence, with a broken relationship, say, 'The glass is broken, it can't be repaired.' But she was wrong. Things cannot be made as they were, but they can become something else. They can be re-made. All things are impermanent, and everything wears down to dust. Everything has its end and each thing carries the beginning of the next thing. Healing is not about re-making things as they once were, healing is about acceptance and forgiveness and love and growth and beginning again. Scar tissue is an inevitable part of life.

The closer things are to being nothing, the more tender they become, and the more tender are the feelings they bring out: a newborn child, a hatchling, a dying old man. A dried seed head surrounded by others; a skeletal leaf floating on a pond; a piece of broken pottery in a pile of soil; half an eggshell lying on the grass; a small bone from a rabbit's leg lying in the sand dunes. Small things that are near their end.

A whole story explodes out of these things. The preciousness in the drying seed head is tied up in the sadness of its turning to dust, and there's joy in the seeds of its offspring showing in the spring. Beauty is a balance between sadness and joy, and is created in the moment, in the relationship between the viewer and the thing viewed. My life is full of this. Such feelings are never in the past or the future, they are only ever here in the inter-action between you and this moment.

A thousand morning sparrows (I know them)
murmuring, wait for warmth
in a leafless tree

a patch of rain so small
that I walk into it and out the other side
looking back I see it still there
over the meadow

then, clear sky, two planes scrape high
trails. A small bird flits through tiny flying insects
and the single scratchy cloud fades away

In the distance a fox yelps
bright chattering birds fling themselves
from one bent hawthorn
to another
and back

and a cat creeps
watching me crouch
in the uncut grass
on my knees as if praying
in a thistle-speckled field

in my hands
a limp blue mole
its soft back snapped
in the steel trap.

Finding and Kneeling

My tunnel probe is a steel rod about 10mm in diameter and 30cm long, with a T-handle at one end, and is ground to a point at the other. I have used a pointed wooden stick from time to time when I have lost my probe in the long grass, but the feedback from a stick is less positive and makes life harder. I painted my probe bright pink so I could see it easily, but it didn't make any difference – the paint wore off and I still lose it.

I look carefully at the nearest scatter of molehills. The fresh ones are in a little group: this is the active area where the mole is feeding. On either side of the hedge there is a cluster of older molehills that could be part of the same territory, and there is a line of ancient, overgrown hills under the hedge which may be a main tunnel.

Squinting at this grouping, I imagine a vague twisting network of tunnels roughly joining all of these features together. I try to imagine where the tunnels might be. Imagination is of great importance when hunting a mole, but it needs to be unclear and uncertain for it to be of any use. You need to imagine a general area, and allow the image to move about and change, rather than try to predict a specific point where a tunnel might be.

Because of the arrangement of the mole-hills – spreading from both sides of the hedge – there could be a main tunnel some-where underneath it, so I probe here first. The best place to put a trap is in a main tunnel, if you can find one, and these will be found somewhere around the perimeter of the active area of molehills, often along a fence line or under the drip line of a hedge. However, the earth in such places is often full of roots, and the tunnels can be difficult to get at.

I walk quietly, even on tiptoe, carrying a set trap with me. Nevertheless, the mole prob-ably has a good idea of where I am. Moles are generally silent: they can scream and cheep, but are rarely heard by humans, and their movements make no sound that I have ever heard, although I know that they can hear me coming from a long way off. I have watched a molehill moving at the limit of my vision and then, as I take a step, it instantly stops.

I push my probe into the ground, feeling for a bump as I break through the tunnel roof and hit the floor. Usually in well-cultivated country earth I can easily push my mole probe into the ground for its full length. Suburban gardens, on the other hand, are often built on waste and rubble and the soil, shipped in from a supplier and tipped on the ground, may be no more than four inches deep. I move slowly and quietly around the area that I feel is going to be fruitful, not expecting any straight lines, probing as I go. I am hunting, and feel the need to be respectful of this process, to quieten my mind and open up my senses.

Molecatchers develop a sixth sense about tunnels. For them it is almost like dowsing. Many times I have wandered around a field for a while and found a good tunnel the first time

I probed. There are subtle cues – too subtle to describe – more a feeling: a tiny difference, perhaps, in ground texture, or springiness when I walk on it; a difference in sound when I walk; the grass lying differently, perhaps, often being more obvious in the morning when it is wet with dew. All these things come together, too tiny to be consciously aware of, but existing just enough for the subconscious to spark an inner voice that says, 'Probe here.' A quiet mind and emotional peace is all-important.

Peggy calls me 'the finder', she says that I am an expert at finding things. Whenever she loses anything – a key, perhaps, or some implement or other, she will tell me about it and I will find it. We both pretend I have a special skill, but really, I think, it is about just finding stuff for her that she can't be bothered to look for.

I have heard it said that there is no point setting traps in between molehills, but I make many catches there; the tunnels by fresh mole-hills are easiest to find and are in active use. There is no point putting a trap actually in a molehill: a mole may sometimes revisit one, but only when the tunnel needs repairs.

I continue to walk quietly and keep probing, stopping, turning around, testing the ground. I am looking for a tunnel that is no more than eight inches deep. I find a number of tunnels that are deeper, so I move on. I won't waste time or energy setting deep traps; it disturbs so much earth that the mole would sense the disturbance and backfill the tunnel. It is much easier to track down a shallower section of tunnel.

In between the hedge and the first fresh molehill I feel my probe break through the roof and drop to the floor of the tunnel with a tiny bump. The depth is good, about five inches. I probe around it, trying to work out which direction it is going in. The more I use my body and feel, and the less I think, the more successful I usually am. Hunting is a two-way process: the earth communicates directly with my body, with my tiniest senses that verge on nothingness.

Having found a tunnel, I am ready to set my first trap. I usually look for between three and five good trap sites for each active territory. I carry lots of traps, and get paid for each mole I catch, so I need to catch them as soon as possible or my bills do not get paid. Relative to his size, a mole's network of tunnels is about the same size as my village is to me. If we were to run every street, every tunnel, I imagine it would take mole and me a couple of hours. I don't run any more, and I don't think that moles saunter.

I kneel in the long grass and arrange my tools. The horizon is green around me, the sun is low over the hills, and there are rooks silent in the trees.

When you don't have the resources that a permanent home provides, things like clean clothes, adequate food of a decent quality, good sleep, plenty of water to drink and wash in, the process of dying speeds up a little, and eventually I started to notice her creeping closer. The time came when I felt she was too close too often, and I knew that I needed to escape while I still could. Eventually a plan developed in my head, and that plan was this: I would carry on doing what I was doing until it got too cold, and then I would head for the coast. And as the rosehips started to redden and the blackberries ripened and the weather turned and the temperature started to fall and the days grew shorter and I could smell the winter coming, I knew it was time to head back to town, find a job, earn some money. I reached the sea and slept on beaches, in the sand dunes, and then the cold weather really came, and I walked down the coast and eventually into Blackpool, a place I had lived in when I was a child, and was pretty certain that I would be able to find work.

I slept under the central pier until I found a job in a warehouse selling tat for the tourist trade. I had not seen my own face for months and was surprised at my appearance: I hadn't started shaving yet but my uncut hair had gone blonde in the sun and somehow, although I rarely washed, I seemed pretty clean. But I was very skinny, and my hunger had moved on from pain to a point that I thought might be dangerous, because I didn't feel hungry any more and I could feel my body breaking down.

I met some hippies who had a flat I could curl up in. I also found my first girlfriend, and I seem to remember sleeping an awful lot. There were drugs in the flat, but I did not need or want them: I had had exhaustion, and days and nights watching small things flit over vast, slow-moving water under a sinking sun; I had seen everyday things that had turned out to be spectacular. I did not need alcohol to make me drunk or numb my senses – I'd had hunger sometimes enough to make me giddy, and freedom enough to make me sing aloud on riverbanks and single-track roads at night. I just needed rest and food, and perhaps the odd hot drink.

I am always looking down

I see the toad and pheasant hiding in the grass
and before I even see it
I know that there's a fox that waits to let me pass

the labyrinth means I can't get lost
but walking I can lose myself
and meet the beast within

the sun is as high as it will get, my shadow is as
    small
swallows and two crows twist
above my silent head

eyeball to eyeball the old fox snakes
through long grass and we look
and see each other's peaceful recognition
and we move on

walking there is nothing

the inescapable destination

wearing horns and grass.

a dog barks

birds sing

insects

horses and their flies.

181

Setting the Traps and Leaving

The mole has a sensitive nose like a dog. My hands are grey and dirty, having been washed with the earth from a molehill. I want my hands to leave no human scent. I want to be part of the background. If it is muddy I wear gloves, but I would rather not. The traps are never washed or oiled, they are often coated in earth, apart from the trigger mechanism, which is brushed clean of anything that would slow it. They are checked for efficiency every time they are set. I want them to smell like the earth.

Using my old sharp spade, I quickly dig straight down and lift back a flap of turf the same width and length as the mole trap. The soil here is dark and slightly sandy, and I am on my wet knees. I break the earth, cutting into whatever is down there that I cannot see:

insects, worms, roots. I put my spare hand on a thistle unseen in the grass and I am stung.

I keep the hole nice and clean. I press down to firm the tunnel floor with the back of my knuckles, and pull out a few bits of grass and earth that have fallen in from the sides where I dug. I look into the tunnel opening on either side of the hole. Push my fingers into the dark tunnel and pull out bits of earth that have rolled down. Trying to make it look undisturbed. Sometimes I can see white hair-like grass roots hanging down inside the tunnel if it isn't extensively used. But grass grows quickly and the mole will probably come back that way again. This tunnel is clear and well used. I can look down it. It is tight with compacted soil in the walls, not shiny-smooth but firm and worn and black, with no loose soil or bits. The base of the tunnel is about six inches below the surface of the soil; it is round, tubular, slightly flattened on the floor. Just like a London Tube train tunnel, but only about six centimetres in diameter.

I put my stainless steel trap into the tunnel.

*

A hunter of any kind needs to learn the arts of hiding specific to his quarry. Invisibility is the greatest skill, one I learned as a child and perfected as a vagrant.

I try to make it look as if nobody but the mole has been here. This all needs to be done quickly: the tunnel is flooding with fresh air and the mole knows his home has been broken into. He is hunkered down somewhere. If I have to delay for any reason, I put my muddy hat down over the hole until I am ready. I work fast, put the trap in place, press the catching loops into the earth on the floor of the tunnel to check the fit. Pull it out again and clear the fallen bits of soil, then put it back into the neatly fitting hole and cover it quickly with loose earth from a molehill.

I am careful not to impede any moving part of the trap with a weight of soil. I want a fast-moving trap, I do not want the mole to suffer, but I don't want air and light to get in, so I cover it with just a light scattering of dry earth. I place the flap of turf gently over the hole so that I can replace it later. Lastly I push a little flag into the ground by the trap so

I can find it again. I get up off my knees and move on, kicking down any molehills as I go, so that the next day I will be quickly able to spot any fresh ones, and see where the mole was working while I was away.

I set my traps quickly; if I work fast he will not have time to work out what is going on, and will settle down that much more easily afterwards. I do not want the mole to get so suspicious that he moves off to another area. If he did that I would have to start all over again. I try hard to give him the world he wants, the one he expects and feels comfortable in. Like a spy or a conman setting up a mark. I give him his routines, make my traps invisible, normal and banal – it is easier to catch a relaxed and careless victim. A mole that others have tried and failed to catch becomes wary and is harder to catch, but I am patient and I will get him.

At my next trap site I make a mess. There is a tree root in the earth, and I have to dig around and cut through it with the secateurs that I keep on my belt. It takes time; air is flooding in. I have a choice now: I can abandon the hole and fill it in, or I can carry on. It is too late, really: the mole will probably be aware of what direction the air is coming from and may already be blocking the tunnel. I decide to place the trap anyway in case I am wrong. I go away quickly, to be somewhere else and be calm. I want the alerted mole to treat the whole event as an aberration, a threat that came and then went. I'm hoping he will sit low, take his time to relax a little. I move quietly away, almost on tiptoe, and plant a trap somewhere else, then somewhere else. I am trying to surround him with traps. Perhaps he may spot the obvious and messy trap site, feel smug at his cleverness and push the trap out of the ground, dig around it or stuff it with earth. Then, thinking that he had solved the problem, dealt with the intrusion that he had become aware of, he would confidently yet devastatingly wander into another of the traps I have set for him. But that is just my fantasy.

I have hidden the grey metal trap with its loops and hooks and springs and triggers in the dark sandy soil, and I must wait for it to do its damage. It will wait and then snap, and a life will be ended, a creature broken and mangled beyond repair. There will be no putting it back together. It will just be tossed away and the crows will eat it. I have become part of the food chain.

The pottery fragment I picked up earlier is still in my pocket; it makes me think of family, me, Peggy, our children who are away and have lives of their own. Fragmented parts of something that was once just one thing. It is triangular, and shaped and sized almost perfectly to fit between two of the three big creases in the palm of my left hand. Again I am struck by how often nature repeats itself.

I am starting to build a new life. I have learned the skills to let go without feeling loss. This jacket, made from spun and woven fleece from sheep fed on grass just over there. Twisted into yarn by people with faces and languages like mine or similar. It's warm and worn against my skin, and smells of lanolin and earth and is the colours of the land. It will rot and become soil. Alive, I blend in; dead, I will blend in. Wearing natural stuff that has grown from the earth, I am connected through my skin and working with nature to keep it alive. It keeps me warm and, as the winter's grip tightens, everyone who works the land can feel it in their core and in their twisting life force that the time to celebrate approaches. This woollen jacket around my shoulders will one day fall to holes, but at this moment it is a warm jacket around my shoulders. It will soon be time to stop, maybe for ever, maybe until next winter comes around.

This is a good life for a man like me.

The light is fading now already, and it is time for me to head home. My house is empty; Peggy is away.

By the end of February the hippies I was squatting with had started to make me nervous. I was grateful to them, but there was squabbling amongst them, and so I decided to wrap up and take off. I had new plimsolls and socks, and a pocket full of money from my job in the warehouse, and I wandered again, up the coast and seaside towns, and then inland through some small country towns for a change. My confidence as a vagrant had grown, and I was not ashamed of being dirty any more. Nevertheless, much of my walk was the same as the previous year: country, riverside, seaside, roadside and woodland, but a point came around mid-summer when my clothes were falling to pieces and I realised that my teeth were bad. When wild animals lose their teeth, that is their end. I needed to get tidied up, find a home and build a different kind of life, so I walked to Manchester and searched out distant family and made them close.

It took me a few months. I took my time, but after a few false leads I found my mother's mother by knocking on doors in the streets I thought I recognised from years previously. She opened the door, let me in, ran me a hot bath, made me a fried egg and chips, and didn't ask me a single question about where I had been. I was a few months off eighteen years old. The next week I was in an office in Manchester Piccadilly railway station being interviewed for a job working in a signal box. I worked on the railway for the next seven years, and then left to go to art school. I had my teeth fixed and one of them replaced with gold.

In bringing out these tarnished memories there is a temptation to polish them up, rub them on a sleeve and make them bright again. But they are old and broken with bits missing, and I don't want them any more. They have earned their patina, and should be left as they are, thrown back in the drawer. Thinking and writing about these events has made me bring my history into the present and I have been having bad dreams. It is time to step out of the grimy past; the past is against my nature, I don't live there.

I have slept by silent death and woken many
    times
it's only life that bites and screams
I have seen it in the fields and woods and hedges
I have delivered it hundreds, maybe thousands
    of times
but will receive it just the once

nature is not kind
the old badger loses its teeth and slowly starves
and as he lies limp and breathing his last few
    breaths
the rats nibble at his tender parts.
I have seen
an old fox freeze to death at the base of a bare
    tree
with worn-out hips
I have seen
the newborn lamb's eyes pecked out by crows
before he even learns to stand
I have squatted near and watched it happen
I've seen the bones
the flesh has lost its glamour

death lives close with those who live in nature
silent yet not cold
the temperature of the earth around
or warm, the warmth of blood
he is nothing to fear
he is the nothing that teaches me to live
to drink and love and sing and dance
in my own mad simple way

until one day he will come
and this capricious anarchic love will end
and like a benevolent father
he'll take me home to my mother

If life is love, then so is death
I fall in love constantly.

Killing

Imagine a steel bar about as thick as your father's thumb hitting you across the chest above your heart at the speed of a rifle bullet. Your ribcage crashes in and your heart stops instantly.

When he enters the trap, the first thing the mole will feel is something hanging down like a root. He'll attempt to push past it. That is also the last thing he will feel. As he pushes it, the hanging wire trigger swings out of the way, a tiny, sensitive hook at the other end of a long lever moves slightly and releases the pin holding the massive spring, which pulls the loop of thick wire out of the ground below him at explosive speed. It is all levers and springs. The distance between the trigger that he presses with his nose and the loop of steel that kills him is tuned to allow the loop to hit him over the heart and kill him instantly. Sometimes a fast mole will get further into the trap before it triggers: caught around his abdomen, he will die more slowly – in a few minutes, perhaps.

The next morning I walk the field to check the traps. I take my trowel with me, I might need it. The flags and a few new molehills appear over a low ground mist. I walk gently to each trap, and with my hand I brush the loose soil off to see if it has sprung. If it has, I pull it out.

In the site that I messed up the trap has sprung. I pull it out and there is a lump of soil that the mole has pushed into the trap. The mole realised that something had encroached into his world and decided to dig around it or under it and rejoin his tunnel further on. It doesn't matter. I kneel down, clear the trap, tidy the hole and reset it as if it were a new site. There may be little point doing this, as logically the mole should not return to this part of his tunnel. He thinks he has blocked it and it doesn't exist any more; it's in the past, and he has created a new route. But catching moles demands a certain amount of magical thinking, and I have caught moles this way. Perhaps they are just too curious for their own good, or maybe they do not know about the past.

In the same territory I pull out another trap that has sprung. There is a mole in it. He is likely to be the mole that discovered the first trap and blocked it. He is caught around his heart, cold and dead. He probably entered the trap within a few hours of me placing it; he will have died the instant he wandered in. I press down on the spring, let his body fall to the ground, reset the trap and replace it, in case another mole enters the now-vacant tunnel, and anyway I can't be bothered to take the trap back. I will leave it in the ground until it is time to take all the traps away. I have to use my mole probe as a walking stick to help me get up – my back aches from years of kneeling and bending. When I come back tomorrow there should be no new molehills in this territory, and no sprung traps. I put his body in my bag and move on to the next territory, the next trap site.

Sometimes I lose a trap to a badger or fox who, smelling quarry, will dig it out. There is an obvious mess, and sometimes I am lucky enough to find the empty trap further down the field in the rough.

Occasionally during the breeding season I will pull out a trap that's caught two moles. They will always be face to face as if approaching to kiss but not quite making it, their noses an inch apart. They were sharing a tunnel, perhaps looking for a breeding partner.

There is a dead mole in my hand. Through the muscle in his neck and shoulders I can just feel the short, strong bones of his arms. When I turn him over he flops, cold, in my palm, and there is a faint golden streak down his belly. If I press his belly in a pink sex organ pops out. I have no idea what sex he is; the only way to find out is to cut him open and look for ovaries.

In the past I skinned a couple of moles and preserved the skins, to see if it was something I could do, slitting gently down the belly with a sharp knife, and peeling the skin away from the membrane that encloses the organs. I was careful: there was no blood, just a bald mole. A translucent bag with hard, pink, blood-filled muscle at one end and soft limp blue organs at the other. There was no fat whatsoever, just muscle and organs. The hide is thin, fragile, and after being dried and cured it ends up being about four inches square and translucent. I have two of them in my desk drawer. They have no use. Moleskins used to be prized by furriers back when people wore skins, and some fly fishermen who want to use natural materials still use the fur to tie flies, using just a few hairs at a time to simulate the hairs on a flying insect – a single moleskin will last a fly fisherman many years. Molecatchers of the past could make a decent second income from selling moleskins to furriers. Now their skins are of no value: they have been replaced by eternal plastic fabrics which I often dig up in tattered bits of rag from the earth. Apparently moles are not pleasant to eat, but of course I have never tried.

*

Altogether in this field I catch eight moles today. All the traps are reset, and I will visit them again tomorrow. Again, I kick down the molehills as I leave so I will be able to recognise any new hills. On my way back to my van I take the eight bodies from my bag and throw them into the hedge for the crows.

This isolated job makes me feel like an animal, I have gained so much and lost so much. I have learned my nature, and at the end of each day I go home, shower and put on the mansuit again. Some things can only be expressed through interaction with others; without them there can be no humanity. Only humans show compassion. I am tired of spending my days alone. I am tired of this labyrinth, this solitary walk.

I'm holding in my hand the roughly triangular fragment of pottery that I picked off the molehill. I found it in my pocket this morning. It is blue and white, heavy for its size, thick and clotted creamy white, with a slight hint of blue like you sometimes find in milk, a faint milky blueness. The edge of a plate, perhaps, curved and smooth at the rim, yet sharp and rough at the broken edges. The pattern is faded blue – the remains of flowers, maybe? It is too small to imagine what the rest of the pattern was, it is just a fragment of foliage. It feels ancient. Somebody used it once, a human. Perhaps an old lady ate meat and vegetables off it, or it was displayed in a cabinet until one day it broke and was thrown away.

I want to go home and be with my ladybird who I damaged and who has repaired herself. Our little life of wife and man and cat, where we are free to tend to each other's needs. My family. The words seem strange to me.

A hedgehog
its face poxed, with shiny blue-black bodies
of vile and gorging ticks passed by
I wanted to feel their bodies crush
like blueberries under my thumb
and the hog's living blood squish out
as the parasites died

still, they have as much right to life
as the hedgehog and as me
which is, after all, just chance
to live, or not to live, or die
I let the hedgehog and its crop of ticks go by

This morning's blistered hands
clawlike from all the many hours on a spade
clip on the handle yet again
some pain
but not enough to take away the pleasure
of the wind scented with rain.

The Fortress and the Worm Larder

I said that moles do not live in molehills, but that is not always true. There is a rare and special type of molehill that a mole will live in. Occasionally in the breeding season I have found a very large molehill, perhaps the size of an upturned wheelbarrow, or a sheep. On shallow or waterlogged soil the breeding female, unable to build an underground nest, may build an extra-large molehill and line it with dried grass and leaves. Molecatchers call this a fortress. If you have a fortress in your garden you are very unlucky indeed.

In one small garden I was called in to deal with a mole problem – there in the middle of a flat, English manicured lawn built shallow over builder's rubble looking as though somebody had tipped a barrow or two of fresh earth in the middle of it: an immense fortress. On all sides of the giant molehill were dozens of fresh, very ordinary molehills. A female from the edge of the playing field beyond the fence had installed herself, and males were coming from far and wide. I visited that one small garden day after day, and pulled out twenty-four moles. The whole garden needed digging out and returfing.

The moles will of course return. The densely populated hedgerow on the other side of the fence will ensure a supply of baby moles for many years to come.

A mole has stuff. Not much of it, but it is there: a familiar home with bedrooms, a regular and predictable job cleaning it and gathering food, a larder or two to keep his food in.

Worms have the enviable ability to grow a new head if they lose the one they were born with. This takes around four to six weeks, but while they grow a new head they are unable to dig. In times of plenty a mole will dig a little room in the wall of his tunnel, then gather lots of worms and bite their heads off, leaving them all knotted together in a section of tunnel. We call this the worm larder; it is a fairly common sight. A tunnel system could have any number of worm larders.

Worms, too, are blind, like moles: they can sense daylight in order to move away from it, but can't see anything. They sense the world through tiny hairs on their bodies. Worms are also hermaphrodites.

The winter is starting to bite now, the days are short and wet and I am feeling that I have really had enough. Those wild places that take me are part of me now, they are carved on my skin, in my cells, part of my character but I feel cold. The cold is a new sensation, it has started to bother me. I am a Northerner, and was always proud of my ability to withstand any depth of chill.

These are the days of a family that I want to curl up with. My world is changing, I am accepting things that will never be and embracing things that I never expected: a different kind of freedom, that comes out of the blue where things and people go and leave space, a vacuum to fill. The children that we have made have left the nest and are building their own. Their clothes and technology and books and CDs and dirty dishes and washing machine full of socks, the large cooking pans we used to need to cater for them, the extra wardrobes – are all gone. We can stay out all night if we want. We never have to go home again. There is a new freedom that feels so familiar. The familiar feeling of walking a path through the countryside with nowhere to go, nothing to achieve apart from just to exist in the moment and absorb the greatness all around.

Looking back on my fragmented, misty and incomplete history of broken family, relationships and incomplete events, there was this path to wholeness, a kind of gravity dragging me toward self-repair. Looking forward, it is impossible to see it, but that attraction and the will to survive makes me fall onward and forward, the cracks slowly filling behind me. At the end of each day I feel full, and perhaps this is more than just acceptance of change, perhaps this is another 'becoming'.

So I look again at this field surrounded by the now dried stalks of cow parsley and the brambles and the ripples in the river flowing next to me, and I think about walking, just putting one foot in front of the other, over and over again.

The woods behind are filled with birdsong rising
above the white noise of windblown leaves
that comes in waves like foam on peaks
of blue green autumn sea

and I remember
I remember when you were sunshine
and I would throw you up in the air
for you to shine down on me
you were always in the air
you were always star-shaped

far behind the you
that you have now become
there's the you that I knew
from the days of picking shells and Lego
arguing about food and bedtimes and clothes
    and school and mess
and I wonder what I will leave behind

there's the you that I do not know
the others in your life and how you feel
you seem to need so little from me now
but still I need to give

you have the careless brutal energy of a market
filled with colour and unplanned meetings
of neighbours haggling over oranges
content to just watch, I see you moving

you see it as onward, I see it as away
I want to tell you how short the road is
but that's not for you to know, not just yet
and I don't want to give you empty weight

instead I want to give you feathers
I show you every day my love for your mother
I have seen how it makes you smile
when Peggy and I laugh together

and hold each other
I hope that can be enough
there's little else to leave behind
not much stuff.

The History of
Molecatching

The European mole is common throughout the UK and most of Europe. Moles are ancient creatures that evolved from shrew-like ancestors 45 million years ago, and dug around under woolly mammoths, big cats and the ancestors of the Neanderthals. Our mole, *Talpa europaea*, has been here eating worms since before the Ice Age. The worms have been here very much longer.

The British Isles saw the first molecatchers around 54BC: they were Romans who didn't want their grapevines and other crops uprooted by moles: they wanted to grow unspoiled flower gardens. There have been molecatchers ever since. I catch moles in the same way that the Romans caught them, by learning their behaviour, probing for tunnels, kneeling down and setting a trap. The reasons for catching them are the same. The only difference is that the trap is slightly more evolved.

In the Middle Ages molecatchers were vagrants who travelled from town to town looking for molehills on people's land, knocking on doors and catching moles for money. Some early molecatchers were seen to have almost magical powers: they traded as wise men and healers, selling talismanic mole hands and skins, making and selling potions. In an age when any infestation could be seen as the work of jealous witches they were cunning men who could devise traps using just sticks and string to catch Mouldiwarp the Earth Shifter, the dark and hidden, seemingly eyeless, earless, genderless devastator of crops.

The medieval molecatchers moved from farm to farm, from village to village. Sometimes they travelled with a horse and caravan, but often just walked with a pack and pole, sleeping in hedgerows as I did as a boy. Perhaps my own journey was inevitable. Their pole was sharpened at one end to probe the ground, and had a small flat spade at the other to dig into the tunnel. They would hang the bodies of the trapped moles on fences or bushes so the farmer would know how many to pay for. Something that still happens in some rural places today; I have done it myself. Sometimes a crow or a fox takes the bodies from the fence and the catcher wouldn't get paid for them, or a badger would dig up a trap and take it. It is all part of the job.

Molecatchers have always been well paid. A Victorian molecatcher would receive an annual salary from the community. He could work for several parishes at once, and some of them became very wealthy. Molecatchers kept their skills well guarded, to protect their trade and expand their territory, and were not above passing on misinformation if pressed.

In living memory itinerant molecatchers would travel from farm to farm, bringing news from neighbouring villages. I have a neighbour, daughter of a Welsh farmer, who remembers the molecatcher, the *'twrchwr'*, coming: he would be fed at the farmhouse and offered a bed until his work was finished.

I go into the field for the third time to check the traps. There are no new molehills. The job is done. I charge a fixed price for every mole I catch. If I don't catch anything I don't charge anything. This never happens. I can give the customer his bill, rake out any molehills that remain, and pull out all the traps. I begin to walk down the field and pull out the traps, starting with the closest. There is no internal journey, no labyrinthine walk, no animal, just a man pulling bits of metal out of the ground and knocking the soil off them, collecting up the bodies. Finishing the easy part of the job and wanting to go home and get warm. Have a whisky, cuddle up. I pull out five more dead, cold moles.

One of the traps I pull out is holding tight around his belly a mole that is still living, squirming to get away. He will have internal injuries, he will die. If I do not do anything, he will die slowly. I have no choice.

My heart races, and I feel unaccountably angry at the mole for not being dead. Not at all happy with what I have to do now. Frustrated that my lovely world has been broken, my pleasure in the job stripped away. I release him from the trap, let him fall to the ground where he writhes, and I have to kneel down next to him and quickly beat him across the head with the back of the trowel. I have to whack him hard five times before he is dead, a trickle of blood from his nose.

I had been feeling for a while that some kind of change was coming, and I knew immediately that this was it. This would be the end of my molecatching. I had rarely had to kill anything without using a machine that did it for me quietly in the night. When I wasn't there. I felt myself to be a hypocrite and a coward. I was upset, sad. I had never deliberately killed anything with my bare hands before, never a mammal anyway, never anything bigger than a mosquito. Though why it should make a difference I would prefer not to think.

I got up, cursed, threw its body into the hedge as if it had just offended me. I felt that I had just stepped out of my familiar world and into a completely new one where I did not really know who I was any more, I wasn't the molecatcher. The oxygen flooded into my tunnel.

Oddly, my next feeling was one of freedom. I felt liberated, from the labyrinth. Everything changed, just as it had changed when I set out with my rucksack all those years ago. Suddenly I was actually thankful to the mole I had just killed. I was confused, but as I left the field I said 'Thank you' to the dead mole, and wondered what had just happened to me. When you have caught the thing that you are looking for it ends. Perhaps sometimes it is better just to hunt and not to catch.

It is growing dark but I feel a lightness, as if this were something I have been waiting for, and I think about why I started catching moles in the first place, my struggle to justify killing, and I remember wondering in the past if it was something that I was capable of doing, and if it might help me to understand more about the kind of man I am.

I still do not know what kind of a man I am. I don't think it matters any more. There is no certainty, only experience. Perhaps everything is just an excuse, and in the end we just choose to believe what we want to believe.

The day is finishing. The farmer has left his tractor at the top of the field and is walking down the fence line toward me. His shape becomes farmer, becomes a whole and complete and rounded man in my world with a ram's-horn stick, and I become a man in his world. I watch him: his walk, his stoop, his clothes, his splash of white hair, his age, and he must see the same things about me. Our different worlds align, and I become aware of being just a man: no horns, no labyrinth, just a muddy man, aware of my height and size, beard and baldiness, the dirt on my clothes and hands.

Even before we make eye contact we are communicating with each other, subconsciously assessing, categorising from appearance and walk, and making judgements about social class and income and lifestyle, and inferences about politics and philosophy and beliefs. Then he has a hand to shake, and a smile and a voice, and we open our mouths to each other and we speak in our own words in our own different accents, and that almost completes the picture, and none of the other stuff matters.

This is the first man I have seen for days, and we talk about climate change, and roses blooming in December, and winter not being winter any more, and am I not cold without a jacket? He leans on the gate and tells me about how it used to be. He'd milked a herd by hand with his gang of mates. But his village is silent now during the day: all the BMWs and Range Rovers are parked in town; the farms are now just people's gardens. His is the only farm that is still productive. His chimney is full of bees. He is lonely, though he didn't say as much. He wanted to know what Facebook was – his grandkids just laughed when he asked. I told him it wouldn't help.

I show him some dead moles, charge him for thirteen. I don't count the live one that I caught: that one was for me, just for me. He counts out the cash. We shake rough hands and go our ways. I feel so much momentary love for him as I watch his bent, tweed-clad back plod back up the hill toward his tractor. I throw the blue bodies into the hedge where the crows will eat them. I like the crows.

Our two worlds having collided and having shared a bit of each other, we slowly drift apart to get on with our tasks and forget, for the most part, the other. Perhaps feeling a little warmth. My solitude, having been broken, is now harder to settle into, but a robin comes and sings to me just an arm's length away. There is always a robin, or a blackbird. The sun is sinking, reminding me that my day's work is short, but the night is long and Peggy will be home. Things have changed. Rain is coming. Dark heavy clouds.

I hold the fragment of pottery in my pocket and I press the point into my thumb.

I dig it in, it hurts a little bit. It is an enjoyable feeling, more discomfort than pain. This piece of history from the ground, digging into my hand, somebody else's memory, not mine. It is nice when it stops, I throw it into the hedge, I am done with it. I am done with breaking things. I am done with history. I am done with digging in the earth.

The stream rocks over stones by the barn and sheep and a field of kale, and at last the rain starts to come. While down the hill the town lights light and the short winter day becomes the night, and I follow it winding down, becoming a different beast with a different prey. Bats fly by eating flying things around my old cold head, and I think of a hot meal and a whisky and I think about Peggy and our bed.

I watch the town light up for a while and feel the conflicting related feelings of love for this life and sadness, then head, in twilight, to my parked van and dump my muddy tools and bag of traps in the back, and drive off through a starting thunderstorm down narrow lanes through villages with pure Welsh names. Heading into the shadows as the day ends. Home to *cwtch*[1] with my ladybird, and to tell her that I am not a molecatcher any more.

---

[1] *Cwtch* is an ancient Welsh word meaning cuddle, comfort or hold. The Old English word 'cotch' meaning to relax is derived from it.

I've cut off my horns that tore her
polished the stumps to mirrors
so she can see how beautiful she is

I turn away again from the fiction of memory
from the melancholic stories of the past
to the easy truth of standing in a wet field
at dusk, before the face of nature
in the distance over field and hedge
a mountain, cloud, a sliver of light
and I feel, for a moment
that this is quite enough

on an ancient fortress hill where sheep lean
and Celts once painted their skin
and rooks reel and cattle watch, chewing
I am perhaps in my last decade on this earth
inescapably drawn toward the end
I follow the call without fear
happy and ready to go home

the truth hides in tiny things
a beetle walks across my still hand as I sit
on the stump of a tree I watched fall
three full years ago

brown now and almost completely decayed to
     crumbly earth
and truth explodes violently
screaming out of this seed
curled frosted leaves the colour of my Peggy's
     hair
applaud the breeze

the sky glows yellow with storm and I welcome
     its coming
it is time for me to look and wait and enjoy the
     waiting that
when it passes will have seemed to have gone too
     soon
the blue moles cold in their traps can wait
the dry rattling seed-headed stalks can wait
the still bright grass can wait
the brambles and the beech hedge and the apple
     trees can wait
I am going home.

The Future

Molecatchers have reappeared in the last few years. If I go online I can find loads of them, where before there were very few. Some of us were taught by the few remaining traditional catchers, others have been on courses. At the last report there were about 300 registered molecatchers in the UK, and there is an ongoing war about membership, legislation and training between the different registration bodies, organisations who exist to make a living off these sole wanderers by forcing them to fit into a modern, regulated world. I was a member of a couple of them for a while, but I am not a person who does membership of things for very long.

Molecatchers are back because strychnine has been outlawed, and untended farmland, modern farming practices and greenfield building means that moles are seen where previously there were no people to see them:

in grass verges along motorways, in suburban gardens, school playing fields and around sports pitches where before there were only fields.

The yellow diggers and bulldozers have already moved into some of my old mole-hunting grounds, and the moles have moved out until it goes quiet. Then they will come back, and people buying new-build houses will find their lawns erupting, and they will have to live alongside all the different kinds of wildlife that were there previously. Moles love the worm population that comes from a well-tended lawn, and until people learn to embrace a bit of wildness in the nature outside their back door, molecatchers will continue to thrive.

A fine-looking garden is a sterile place. A perfect green lawn is only kept that way by continually dosing it with chemicals. A lawn that is not treated will naturally become home to a massive number of species of birds and worms and native wild plants, crane-fly larvae, beetles, invertebrates. There are people who do not want living organisms in their gardens, and they spray their lawns with chemicals that kill the worms so there are no worm casts, moles or birds pecking at the grass, then they spray it with chemicals to kill the crane-fly larvae so there are no magpies, jays or crows digging up the grass to get them, and so there will be no daddy longlegs in the summer; in the spring they spray it with chemicals to reduce the growth of the grass so they do not have to mow it so often and other chemicals are used to kill the moss and weeds and make the grass greener. For some, even mowing is too much, so they pay to have the grass stripped off and replaced with plastic grass that you can smell as it warms under the hot summer sun and will last until the world ends.

I was for a while the only registered mole-catcher in my area. I gave it up this year, but keep getting calls from potential customers new and old. I have read that the mole population in the UK could number between 30 and 40 million and rising, because arable farmers no longer need to catch them. When the gardeners call with their pleas to come and get rid of their moles, I tell them that I have retired. When they ask what they should do about the moles I tell them to learn how to do it themselves, or to grow a flower meadow, which I will happily come and advise them on. For a fee.

The moles don't need to be killed. The European mole is a protected species in Germany and Austria: gardeners there put up with them.

I have no future in molecatching, and although it has given me a life that I have loved – a small life, not much – it is a life hand-made by me. I am not a master craftsman, but out of something ill-formed, worthless and unwanted, like a Japanese potter I filled the cracks with gold. I do not know what life is, but I know what it does. Molecatching has been a life that has brought me closer to the nature of my own existence, and what it means. It has allowed me to treat the wild outside as a precious home, instead of something one is cast out into. To feel directly connected to the breath of the air that fuels me, to the soil and the sun and the rain that feed me. It has made me fit and healthy and peaceful. That connection with the earth is now part of every cell of my body, but I need to rest. It has been an isolated life at times, I have been an outsider and lost many of the few communication skills I ever had. I crave the company of human beings, even though I am nervous about how to relate to them. I am tired. I have ten more years, perhaps, before I am too frail to dance at a party with others. I want to join in, and so this life is at an end for me, and I am starting another one.

I am tired of looking for hidden things; the things that matter are all there, just to be had, lying on the surface. The fragments that I can hold and carry with me. The hidden things can remain where they are, because their truth too is hidden and vague and unfathomable to be of any daily value.

Driving narrow lanes by curly bracken banks
where Welsh villages no longer anglicise their
 names
black sky
fat sleet slaps my windscreen
and chased by thunder I race down
this thin strip of wet black tar
printed on the hillside

home to Peggy through a thunderstorm
crackling with excitement
and singing in the pouring rain

the town down the hill
starts its toxic undark
the evening and I wind down
in misting sleet to rest

and for this sole cold hunter
a log fire a quiet house
a tot with Peggy by the flames
will round the day full circle
this tattooed battered matted iron-bound hand
has one job left to do today

to stroke the soft grooved downy back of her
　　neck

curled under thick quilts
more woodlouse than man
in our soft padded nest
I am quiet
with curtains and windows open
so we can hear the owl and fox at night
and be woken
by the cool red-streaked dawn.

Epilogue

Another morning. Daylight, and waves crashing against the window, a three-inch fog of bouncing grey felts the horizon and confused car alarms call for each other across flooded gullies. Steaming up the streaming glass with a mug of hot chocolate, I press my face to the window. The cat brushes against my ankles, mewling for attention. I am watching blurry bright colours moving through the rain and pondering the possibility of going out. Maybe I will just stay here watching. I can watch for hours, days. There is one month to the winter solstice, the shortest day. I should perhaps eat, and I wonder how I will fill this day. Perhaps I will go and walk in the fields.

Much later.

It is cold now and I have been watching the rain all day long, and the day has come and gone while I watched. Darkness falls. The outside fades and, where just a moment ago I saw trees, I can see now reflected in the window a few things scattered on the beaten sofa where she was: a blanket, a laptop, some junk mail, a cold coffee cup on the floor, and myself. I have stopped fighting to shine a light. We come, we go again. Peggy has gone to bed, and I am still listening to the rain with a whisky while the darkness takes over. A street light flickers on the raindrops on the window in the dark. It is all sparks. Peggy breathes deeply and waits. I can hear the sentinel blackbird singing in the pine outside my window. It sings there every night just as the light fades, and again in the morning before the light returns.

I am watching, unable to tear myself away from my chair, from the window, to leave the sky. I have spent the whole day without purpose, just looking at the white sky. Waiting for snow and wondering what it would be like to walk barefoot in it. I drift off to sleep. A hard shower and gusting wind at midnight wakes me, crackling, static? Did I leave the radio on? A faint laughter? A distant voice calling for help? The noise passes and I go to bed.

The ponderous egg of earth rotates into the light again, and all across the surface bells begin to ring announcing the advancing wave of day. And here in my little bed I wake too from my slow night cruise through the dark. As the shadows of people and trees and buildings crawl across the planet like eyelashes, the day opens, the light comes in. Made from dust from the explosion at the dawn of time. I become aware. Open my eyes. Morning.

The days go by, one after the other, with little changing but the weather and the temperature and the day length. The nights get shorter. The snowdrops come, and then the crocuses, then massed acres of daffodils, and the spring arrives and I find new things to do. Suddenly, as life has become clearly shorter, we have more time. I can allow things to show themselves as they are, rather than trying to bend them to my will.

We wake in a tangled nest
of legs and arms
and hair and beard my ladybird
we wake to precious days
as in the distance we begin to see
the tunnel at the end of the light

pressing my fingers in between
your vertebrae one by one
and holding your round foot
like a child's
you hold me tight
I am a tree wrapped round with ivy

'I love you,' you said
lying there quiet
with my hand on your leg

both wide awake and breathing, listening
the windows open, shutters closed
to the pigeon on the roof
and the market setting up in the square down
    below.

*

This is how my last days as a molecatcher passed. I have pulled up all of my traps, I've put them in a bag in the shed, and they will stay there. I will spend more of my time just looking.

The small things are the things which in their millions make the world work. The craftsmen, the traders, the men in white vans who bring stuff and fix stuff; the people in the factories who knit my jumpers and weave the wool to make the tweed for my trousers; the farmers – the individual men and women who care for and grow the things we eat and wear, who look after the landscape for the love of it. The steps that we take that lead us to where we are. The small things, the tiny, tiny interactions, are the journey.

Nothing is complete, nothing is perfect and nothing is ever finished. I have developed tender feelings toward the unrelenting drive toward entropy that I take with me. It is everywhere and in everything.

*

They pass so quickly
These moments of perfection
Look! Here's another!

My life I hope
A golden leaf that fluttered by
No more or less important
Look! A blackbird eating berries in the tree!

Watching the sun rise
Life goes on. And then it stops
Do try to watch it!

I no longer hide.

Photo taken at the pet cemetery at Nanteos Mansion in West Wales.

235

Acknowledgements

I cannot let a moment go by without thanking my agent, the deeply lovely Robert Caskie of Caskie Mushens, who completely understood what I was trying to do with this book and quickly saw its potential. He helped me to develop my idea into something that somebody else might want to read, and then he and his co-agents and scouts went on to find some marvellous editors across the world who reacted just as positively, especially the incredibly sensitive Elizabeth Foley at Harvill Secker, who not only encouraged and helped me to work it up into the form that you hold in your hand but also included me in the design process and the choice of illustrators, for which I am deeply thankful. I also want to thank the hugely talented Design Editor Suzanne Dean at Harvill Secker for the shape and form of this book and of course Joe McLaren for the beautiful drawings. Thanks to Gemma Osei, and Mikaela Pedlow for your help and to the many, many people whose names I do not know at agencies and publishers who have read this and had a hand in how it looks and how it reads; I am deeply grateful.

Special thanks must go to Oscar, who put up with me sitting at his dining table to work on this, and to Erica, who let me sit in her cottage away from all distractions while the wind battered away at the walls and I burned her logs and finished the first drafts. There were some lovely people who chose to turn away and not say anything while, instead of working in their gardens for an hourly rate, I was making notes for this book or writing poetry, or looking at spider webs or piles of leaves in a distracted poety kind of way and who, disgracefully, I abandoned because I had a book to finish writing. Jean and Sal, Rhys and Sue, Maria, Peter and Wendy, Izabella, Judy, Dena, David and Liz – thank you.